ICNC **MONOGRAPH** SERIES

SERIES EDITOR: Maciej Bartkowski
CONTACT: mbartkowski@nonviolent-conflict.org
VOLUME EDITOR: Amber French
DESIGNED BY: David Reinbold
CONTACT: icnc@nonviolent-conflict.org

Other volumes in this series:

People Power Movements and International Human Rights, by Elizabeth A. Wilson (2017)

Making of Breaking Nonviolent Discipline in Civil Resistance Movements, by Jonathan Pinckney (2016)

The Tibetan Nonviolent Struggle, by Tenzin Dorjee (2015)

The Power of Staying Put, by Juan Masullo (2015)

Published by ICNC Press
International Center on Nonviolent Conflict
1775 Pennsylvania Ave. NW. Ste. 1200
Washington, D.C. 20006 USA

© 2017 International Center on Nonviolent Conflict, Dr. Stephen Zunes
All rights reserved. ISBN: 978-1-943271-11-5

Cover Photos: (l) Flickr user Yamil Gonzales (CC BY-SA 2.0) June 2009, Tegucigalpa, Honduras. People protesting in front of the Presidential Palace during the 2009 coup. (r) Wikimedia Commons. August 1991, Moscow, former Soviet Union. Demonstrators gather at White House during the 1991 coup.

Peer Review: This ICNC monograph underwent four blind peer reviews, three of which recommended it for publication. After satisfactory revisions ICNC released it for publication. Scholarly experts in the field of civil resistance and related disciplines, as well as practitioners of nonviolent action, serve as independent reviewers of ICNC monograph manuscripts.

Publication Disclaimer: The designations used and material presented in this publication do not indicate the expression of any opinion whatsoever on the part of ICNC. The author holds responsibility for the selection and presentation of facts contained in this work, as well as for any and all opinions expressed therein, which are not necessarily those of ICNC and do not commit the organization in any way.

Civil Resistance Against Coups

A COMPARATIVE AND HISTORICAL PERSPECTIVE

Honduran people demonstrating in the streets during the 2009 coup d'état. Credit: Flickr user Yamil Gonzales.

Executive Summary

Nations are not helpless if the military decides to stage a coup. On dozens of occasions in recent decades, even in the face of intimidated political leaders and international indifference, civil society has risen up to challenge putschists through large-scale nonviolent direct action and noncooperation. How can an unarmed citizenry mobilize so quickly and defeat a powerful military committed to seizing control of the government? What accounts for the success or failure of nonviolent resistance movements to reverse coups and consolidate democratic gains?

This monograph presents in-depth case studies and analysis intended to improve our understanding of the strategic utility of civil resistance against military takeovers; the nature of civil resistance mobilization against coups; and the role of civil resistance against coups in countries' subsequent democratization efforts (or failure thereof). It offers key lessons for pro-democracy activists and societies vulnerable to military usurpation of power; national civilian and military bureaucracies; external state and non-state agencies supportive of democracy; and future scholarship on this subject.

Major gaps exist in bodies of knowledge that feed into each of the above constituencies' understanding of the civil resistance against coups phenomenon. For example, countries spend massive amounts of resources to prepare for defensive and offensive wars against foreign enemies or suppression of domestic terrorists, but not against the threat of a coup—historically a much greater tangible risk to societal and democratic well-being of nations.

At the same time, the vast majority of the literature on military coups largely ignores the role of civil society, nonviolent mobilization and civil resistance. Studies on coups have been dominated by top-down assumptions of political power, focusing on palace intrigues, governing structures, geopolitical alliances, personalities of leaders, and narrowly defined strategic considerations of key domestic and international elite actors. This monograph attempts to address these gaps by offering a new analytical, category-based and case study-enriched perspective on understanding how civil resistance against coups has worked.

A main practical finding of this monograph is that the goal of pro-democracy resistance against coups should be about defending society, not a particular physical location. The defense of a society threatened by a coup relies on widespread mobilization, building alliances, nonviolent discipline, and refusal to recognize illegitimate authority.

Given that the vast majority of anti-coup mobilization cases examined in this monograph did not have the benefit of extensive pre-planning, it raises the question of how many successful coups in recent years could have been prevented or defeated quickly—providing an even greater boost to post-coup democratization efforts—had the population been prepared and equipped with suitable skills and knowledge of civil resistance.

Table of Contents

Executive Summary	5
Introduction	9
Past Nonviolent Actions Against Coups	10
Analytical and Empirical Questions	12
Six Scenarios of Civil Resistance and Coups	14
Literature on Nonviolent Defense	17
Literature on Coups and Civil Resistance	18
Part 1: Six Coup Scenarios Illustrated Through 12 Case Studies	23
1) Post-Coup Civil Resistance that led to Coup Reversals	23
Soviet Union, July 1991	23
The Resistance	24
The Aftermath	25
Thailand, May 1992	27
The Resistance	27
The Aftermath	28
Soviet Union and Thailand: Comparison and Conclusion	30
2) Preventing the Consolidation of a Coup in Progress	31
France, April 1961	32
The Resistance	32
The Aftermath	33
Argentina, April 1987	35
The Resistance	36
The Aftermath	37
France and Argentina: Comparison and Conclusion	39
3) Defending Newly-won Democracy Against a Coup	40
Bolivia, November 1978	40
The Resistance	40
The Aftermath	41
Burkina Faso, September 2015	44
The Resistance	45
The Aftermath	47
Bolivia and Burkina Faso: Comparison and Conclusion	49
4) Coups Allegedly in Defense of Democracy	49

Venezuela, January 1958 50
The Resistance 50
The Aftermath 52
Mali, March 1991 55
The Resistance 55
The Aftermath 56
Venezuela and Mali: Comparison and Conclusion 60

5) Anti-Democratic Coups Following Civil Resistance-Initiated, Alleged Pro-Democracy Coups 61
Sudan, April 1985 and June 1989 61
The Resistance 62
The Coup and its Aftermath 62
Egypt, February 2011 and July 2013 65
The Resistance 65
The Coup and its Aftermath 66
Sudan and Egypt: Comparison and Conclusion 70

6) Unsuccessful Civil Resistance to Coups 71
Honduras, 2009 71
The Resistance 72
The Aftermath 74
The Maldives, 2012 76
The Resistance 77
The Aftermath 77
Honduras and the Maldives: Comparison and Conclusion 80

Part 2: Generalized Findings from the Analyzed Cases 81

Part 3: Takeaways for Specific Practitioner Groups 93
Activists and Civil Society Groups 93
Building Societal Capacity Against Coups 93
Security Forces and Government Civil Servants 94
External State Actors/International Community 95
This Monograph as an Educational Instrument Against Coups 96

Bibliography 97

List of Scenarios and Tables 102

Introduction

While governments can be brought down through nonviolent civil insurrections, popular legitimate governments can also be overthrown by force through armed minorities, such as through a coup d'état. Some coups come in response to massive popular uprisings against the incumbent regime. Most of the time, however, they are decidedly anti-democratic in nature. In recent years, the world has seen a popular nonviolent uprising reverse a coup within days and restore democracy (Burkina Faso, 2015). It has also witnessed a coup ostensibly in support of a popular uprising that led to the consolidation of a military regime (Egypt, 2013) and successful popular resistance to a coup attempt used by a civilian government to consolidate authoritarian rule (Turkey, 2016).

This monograph examines civil resistance against efforts by the military or other security forces to forcefully overthrow constitutional governments, particularly those seeking to impose autocratic rule. Through examining variations in successful coup resistance, the causal processes of various coup resistances, and the differences between six different kinds of coup resistance, this monograph explores key variables that explain the success or failure of nonviolent resistance movements to reverse coups and consolidate democratic governance. A key finding is that, regardless of the motivation of the coup plotters and the level of success popular forces experienced in defending or restoring democracy, the physical control of government facilities—which is generally the first target of coup plotters—is not the same as the political control of the state.

Over the past few decades, coup plotters in many cases have physically seized control of some key government institutions and declared the incumbent government ousted and themselves the new legitimate state authority—only to find that the majority of the population does not recognize their legitimacy and refuses to cooperate with their orders. In such situations, the plotters find themselves unable to consolidate their grip on power and govern effectively, thereby resulting in the collapse of the coup. The key to understanding this development is the behavior and actions of ordinary people. They either acquiesce to planned, attempted, or successful coups or, on the contrary,

engage in mass-based noncooperation.

The ability to hold state power ultimately depends on the cooperation of both civilian and security personnel employed by the state who are necessary for the state apparatus to function. In addition, even if the putschists (those who take part in a coup or coup attempt) are successful in initially seizing power, they are still ultimately dependent on the willingness of local governments, independent social institutions, and the general population to recognize their authority and cooperate with them.

Civil resistance to coups employs many of the same tactics that have been used by popular unarmed insurrections to topple autocratic regimes. However, the political context is very different. In the hours and days after a coup, the putschists generally have not yet consolidated their control on the instruments of state power, including at least some elements of security forces, so they are far more vulnerable to noncooperation and mass action. However, pro-democracy elements must mobilize quickly and engage in what may be unplanned and largely spontaneous acts of resistance, lacking the time that those in more protracted pro-democracy struggles have to build up organization, cadre, trainers, communication, and other assets that are important to the success of a civil insurrection.

Past Nonviolent Actions Against Coups

The utilization of nonviolent resistance to reverse coups d'état is not a new practice. Nearly a century ago, in March of 1920, a right-wing putsch in Germany composed of soldiers, army veterans, and right-wing civilians occupied Berlin in a coup against the young Weimar Republic. Organized by Dr. Wolfgang Kapp and Lieutenant-General Walter von Lüttwitz, almost all of the German military either supported it or remained neutral. The legitimate government, forced to abandon Berlin, moved to Stuttgart and called on Germany's workers to defeat the putsch by means of a general strike. With strong working-class support, the trade unions—which were sympathetic to the ousted Social Democratic-led government—joined the call for a strike on the same day, as did the major centrist, center-left, and communist parties. In what became the largest general strike in German history, up to 12 million workers nationwide forced the country to ground to a halt. In Berlin, the gas, water and power supply all collapsed. The country's banks refused to provide funds for the putschists. The noncooperation was so massive that putsch leaders couldn't even find any secretaries to type their memos

Introduction

(Sharp and Jenkins, 2003, 10-11).

The reversal of the Kapp Putsch has largely been forgotten as a result of the Nazi takeover of the country 13 years later and—despite a plethora of military takeovers in subsequent decades—no such coup reversals took place again until the late 1970s. Since then, however, there have been more than a dozen such episodes in other parts of the world. Not all have been successful, such as the impressive civil resistance campaigns against the coup in Honduras in 2009 and in the Maldives in 2012 that were ultimately crushed. However, there have now been enough successful cases in which strategic nonviolent action has been used to reverse coup attempts so as to be able to put forward some preliminary analysis of this phenomenon and derive key lessons and takeaways for various stakeholders, including activists and organizers, policy makers, and external actors.

> *Since the end of World War II, 94 countries, constituting over half of the world's governments, have been overthrown in a coup d'état at least once.*

Since the end of World War II, 94 countries, constituting over half of the world's governments, have been overthrown in a coup d'état at least once. This trend has become far less common in recent decades (Powell and Thyne, 2011, 249-259). There could be several factors for this, including the end of the Cold War, during which the Soviet Union and some Western governments competed to bring down regimes that were not to their liking. Western governments began perceiving less of a need to support rightwing autocrats in order to counter leftist influences. Other factors include the growth of global civil society, increasing interdependence between nations, and a wave of democratization, which together seem to be delegitimizing coups d'état.

Another reason may be the success of largely nonviolent civil resistance movements against autocratic regimes. Civil resistance movements generate bottom-up legitimacy and maximize public support. As a result, those leading coups need more material and human resources in order to seize and maintain control of the state. This functions as a deterrent for coup attempts.

Despite this, coups d'état remain a major threat to democratic political systems—far greater than the prospects of a foreign invasion or other external intervention. Ironically, it is the country's armed forces, developed to protect the country from external threats to its security, which are primarily responsible for domestic interference in the form of coups. Moreover, while there have been extensive studies on how a country might resist foreign aggression, little has been written about the threat of coups, even though far more governments have fallen from internal coups than foreign invasions. Even when coups fail, it can have a negative impact on freedom. A Freedom House study in 2016 noted a decline in political freedom and other civil liberties following coup attempts, though most of the coups cited failed for reasons other than civil resistance (Nelson, 2016). As a result, developing an effective deterrent against military coups remains an important goal for defending democracy.

Analytical and Empirical Questions

This monograph seeks to understand how civil resistance has played a role in challenging military coups, in particular: Why do nonviolent resistance movements to reverse coups and consolidate democratic governance succeed or fail?

Each case study examines:

The principal actors:
- Who were the putschists and what were their goals? How did they attempt to seize power?
- Who were the main actors involved in the civil resistance movements? What was their relationship with the elected governments?
- How large and diverse was the movement?
- Who were the movements' allies, domestically and internationally?

Strategies and tactics:
- What major tactics did the resistance movements use? How did these tactics undermine the support mechanisms that would have otherwise led to putschists' successful consolidation of power?
- Was there some level of planning and strategic thinking in the resistance, or was it largely spontaneous?
- What degree of nonviolent discipline did the resistance maintain and how did that contribute to the outcome?

Introduction

Response to the uprising:
- How long did the coup attempt last and how long was the resistance?
- What role did security forces play in supporting pro-democratic forces?
- How severe was the repression?

The impact:
- What were the short- and long-term results of using civil resistance?
- What about cases where the military stages a coup ostensibly in support of a democratic civil insurrection?
- What was the longer-term impact of people-led, anti-coup resistance on the country and the society?

This monograph will seek to answer these questions by examining a dozen cases of civil insurrections related to coups d'état as outlined in six scenarios below.

In measuring some of the key variables (see the summary tables developed for each case study included in later chapters), this monograph considers the following:

1. Level of planning/strategic thought

The ability to plan and think strategically in challenging a coup through civil resistance is relatively limited compared to campaigns against already-existing dictatorships. Still, in the case studies we sometimes observe a degree of strategic thought, such as selection of tactics, targets, demands, building alliances, etc., as well as coordination between groups. "High" would indicate a clear and organized plan of action; "Low" would indicate largely spontaneous actions; "Moderate" would indicate a mixture of spontaneity and strategic planning.

2. Level of nonviolent discipline

"High" would indicate an overwhelmingly nonviolent response with no armed components, rioting, destruction of property, or attacks on security forces, coup officials, or their supporters. "Low" would indicate the utilization of armed elements, large-scale property destruction, and a large percentage of opponents engaged in rioting and other violent actions. "Moderate" would indicate a mostly nonviolent focus along with a minority of elements engaged in violent activity.

3. Level of repression

"High" would indicate large-scale killings of civilians, arrest of oppositionists, destruction of their assets, and other actions that would limit oppositionists' ability to openly organize; "Low" would indicate security forces unwilling or unable to suppress oppositionists; "Moderate" would indicate some arrests and killings of oppositionists but not to the degree that would severely limit oppositionists' organizing ability.

Six Scenarios of Civil Resistance and Coups

In attempting to understand the dynamics of civil resistance (CR) in response to military coups, this monograph will examine six different scenarios consisting of two cases in each identified category.

SCENARIO 1) Cases of countries without recent experience in large-scale civil resistance that undergo a military coup and the coup is reversed through civil resistance:

- **SOVIET UNION, 1991**
- **THAILAND, 1992**

*The arrows indicate that civil resistance is used against the established coup, leading to its eventual collapse.

Introduction

SCENARIO 2) Cases of civil resistance that prevented the consolidation of a coup in progress:

- **FRANCE, 1961**
- **ARGENTINA, 1987**

*The arrows indicate that civil resistance is used against a military rebellion and prevented a full-fledged coup from taking place. This, in turn, paved the way for a subsequent democratic consolidation.

SCENARIO 3) Cases of countries in which a longstanding authoritarian government is ousted through civil resistance, the new democratic government is then overthrown in a coup, yet a new wave of civil resistance soon ousts the newly-formed regime and restores democracy:

- **BOLIVIA, 1979**
- **BURKINA FASO, 2015**

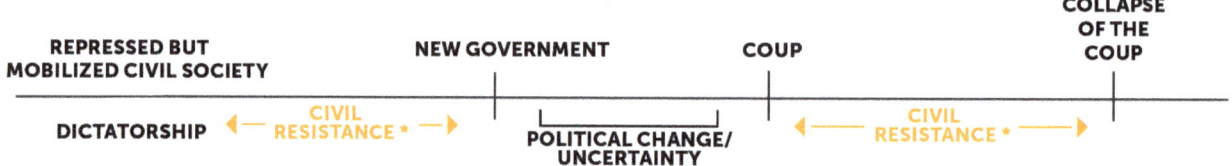

*The arrows indicate that civil resistance is used against a dictatorship that leads to a new government and then against a coup that leads to its eventual collapse.

SCENARIO 4) Cases of countries where coups take place in the name of an ongoing pro-democracy civil resistance campaign and paved the way for democratization with continued civic mobilization:

- **VENEZUELA, 1958**
- **MALI, 1989**

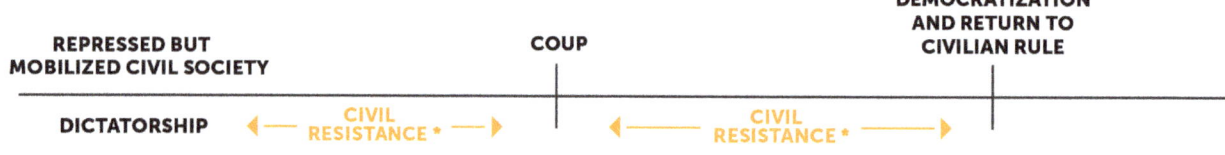

*The arrows indicate that civil resistance is used against a dictatorship that paves the way for a coup. Sustained civil resistance allows for gradual democratization.

SCENARIO 5) Coups that take place in the name of an ongoing pro-democracy civil resistance campaign, that initially allow a democratic opening before consolidating power under a new dictatorship:

- **SUDAN, 1985-1989**
- **EGYPT, 2011-2013**

*The arrows indicate that civil resistance is used against a dictatorship that leads to the fall of an autocrat. During the political uncertainty that follows and ongoing civil resistance against the status quo, the military consolidates its power.

SCENARIO 6) Civil resistance against coups that failed:

- **HONDURAS, 2009**
- **MALDIVES, 2012**

*The arrow indicates that the coup leads to the consolidation of power by the military and the subsequent elections are skewed in its favor.

Each of the above six scenarios provides an opportunity to better understand the strategic utility of civil resistance against military takeovers, the nature of civil resistance mobilization against coups, the role of civil resistance in democratization (or failure thereof), and lessons for pro-democracy activists, members of security services and government agencies supportive of democracy, the international community, and societies as a whole.

This study does not cover a number of coups, including Germany (1920), Japan (1936), Spain (1981), Haiti (1991), Guatemala (1993), Venezuela (2002), Ecuador (2010), and Turkey (2016). Some of these involved significant civil resistance, though in other cases the coups were reversed largely by opposition from elite sectors, including prominent politicians, other elements of the armed forces, and the international community, without significant mobilization from civil society. Even in the latter such cases, however, the prospect of civil resistance or a lack of bottom-up legitimacy for coups may have played a role in influencing certain elites to side with the elected government.

Literature on Nonviolent Defense

Much of the literature examining the theory and dynamics of nonviolent resistance to coups d'état is rooted in studies on nonviolent means of resisting foreign invasion and occupation. During the Cold War, the prospect of mutual destruction encouraged new thinking about nonviolent national defense among security scholars. Building on some early reflections by Bertrand Russell (1915) a century ago, Commander Sir Stephen King-Hall, Theodor Ebert, Adam Roberts, Gene Sharp and Thomas Schelling have since explored the phenomenon of "civilian-based defense" (CBD), also known as "nonviolent defense," "social defense" and "defense by civil resistance."

King-Hall (1958) was the first to present a comprehensive proposal for popular nonviolent resistance as an alternative to military defense, calling for a tough and pragmatic approach to nonviolent action. Sharp (1965) described civilian-based defense as the "political equivalent of war" and wrote about how methods of collective noncooperation and disruptive nonviolent action could be employed as a functional alternative, or possibly as a complement, to traditional defense strategies for resisting external invasion and preventing coups. Roberts (1968) edited a volume that includes several case studies of civilian-based defense (German resistance in the Ruhr [1923], Norwegian and Danish Resistance against German occupation in World War II, and East German resistance against communist rule [1953]). Roberts's study examines how noncooperation with an adversary's orders, popular defiance, attempts to encourage noncompliance among security forces and functionaries, the creation of parallel structures, and other forms of nonviolent action can contribute to national defense.

Boserup and Mack (1974) conducted a study commissioned by the Danish government to analyze the theory of nonviolent defense. It included a number of historical examples, examined strategic and organizational issues, and speculated on the possibility of combining both nonviolent and military methods of defense. Two case studies of civilian-based resistance against foreign occupation are Eglitis (1993) and

Miniotaite (2002), focusing on Latvia and Lithuania, respectively. Each of these studies draws lessons relevant to the broader topic of civilian-based defense. In a study of a much earlier case, Huxley (1990) documents in detail Finnish "passive resistance" against Russia in the late 19th and early 20th centuries.

Sharp (1985) made the case that civilian-based nonviolent deterrence and defense was a viable alternative to NATO's military approach in the face of potential aggression from the Warsaw Pact. A more detailed analysis by Schmid (1985) studied Soviet military interventions and nuclear threats during the previous 40 years and its implications for social defense; four Eastern European case studies of nonviolent resistance and what might have made them more successful; and possibilities of a more comprehensive defense system from a resource mobilization perspective. Sharp also wrote a general overview of civilian-based defense in which he advocates for a process of "transarmament," defined as "the process of changing over from a military system to a civilian-based defense system" (Sharp, 1990, 67). Burrowes (1996) has contributed some important theoretical analysis on the question of nonviolent defense and Bartkowski (2015b) has written about how civilian-based defense can contribute to countering modern hybrid warfare, using the ongoing cases of the annexation of the Crimea by Russia and the conflict in eastern Ukraine.

Literature on Coups and Civil Resistance

The vast majority of the literature on military coups largely ignores the role of civil society and civil resistance. For example, Naunihal Singh's *Seizing Power: The Strategic Logic of Military Coups* (2014)—the most important recent study of the phenomenon—downplays the role of civilians during a military coup and the impact of street demonstrations and mass civil action. Indeed, the literature has been dominated by top-down assumptions of political power, focusing on palace intrigues, governing structure, geopolitical alliances, personalities of leaders, and narrowly defined strategic considerations with little regard to agency and the role of the general population. Even assuming the primacy of elite decision-making, the question of what makes key elite actors decide whether to support or oppose a coup must include an understanding of the role a population may have in influencing their choices.

There is very little literature on nonviolent civic mobilization against military takeovers that can be found in political science, international relations or social movement studies. The few studies that do exist on this subject have been written by civil resistance scholars and practitioners. They either focus on single cases or were published a few decades ago. There is little in the way of systemic analysis on how civil resistance works against coups, nor has there been any cross-country comparisons—omissions that this monograph attempts to rectify.

One of the few attempts to examine this phenomenon came in Adam Roberts's 1975 article from the *Journal of Peace Research*, "Civil Resistance to Military Coups," in which he noted the problems inherent in violent responses to military coups and coup attempts, as well as their limited effectiveness. By contrast, he noted, civil resistance can be particularly powerful since it undermines the very legitimacy of the coup itself:

> Why did these coups fail? Partly, no doubt, they failed because their leaders, like so many military insurrectionists, tended to base their plan of action upon the assumption that the public would rally to them. The curious Spanish term for a military seizure of power, *pronunciamento*, itself indicates a belief that the mere taking up of a position, and the pronouncing of a phrase, would be enough to give one charge of a government. [The failed 1920 German putschist] Kapp and [the failed 1960 French coup leader] Challe both had the common delusion that once they put themselves forward everyone would follow. When people failed to do so and then their own military resources evaporated they lost heart. In cases such as these even token civilian opposition can have a disproportionate effect (Roberts, 1975, 31).

At the conclusion of his article, Roberts (1975, 34) observed:

> What is now needed is the formulation, on the basis of a wider historical survey, of some theories about the conditions for and dynamics of civil resistance against military coups. Such theories might enlarge our understanding of the overall roles of civil resistance in political processes, and illuminate the specific relationships of civil resistance to the threat and use of violence. Such theories might also have a more immediate functional value in contributing to the possibility of survival of certain regimes when faced with the prospect of military usurpation.

Despite this call, issued more than four decades ago, very little research has been done on the role of civil resistance in preventing or reversing military coups. The first and thus far only comprehensive study of this phenomenon came out in 2003 in a monograph entitled *The Anti-Coup* by Gene Sharp and Bruce Jenkins, published by the Albert Einstein Institution. They underscore the importance of distinguishing between the physical control of government facilities and the political control of the state. They note how bureaucrats, civil servants, and other government employees, along with security services that refuse to cooperate with the coup plotters, can deny the latter the ability to control the state apparatus. Even if the coup instigators do manage to obtain control of much of the state apparatus, they cannot control the country if local governments, independent social institutions, and the general population refuse to cooperate. Examining cases from Germany (1920), France (1961), and the Soviet Union (1991), the authors conclude that the key to defeating a coup is denying the putschists what they need to control the country: legitimacy and cooperation. Specifically, Sharp and Jenkins argue that the resisters must aim to:

- Repudiate the putschists as illegitimate with no rightful claim to become the government;
- Make the attacked society unrulable by the attackers;
- Block the imposition of a viable government by the putschists;
- Maintain control and self-direction of their society;
- Make the institutions of the society into omnipresent resistance organizations against the coup;
- Deny to the putschists any additional objectives;
- Make the costs of the coup and the attempted domination unacceptable;
- Subvert the reliability and loyalty of the putschists' troops and functionaries and induce them to desert their mutinous officers;
- Encourage dissension and opposition among the putschists' supporters;
- Stimulate international opposition to the coup by diplomatic, economic, and public opinion pressures against the attackers; and
- Achieve international support in communications, finances, food, diplomacy, and other resources (Sharp and Jenkins, 21).

Introduction

To achieve these initial objectives, Sharp and Jenkins (26-27) argue that the pro-democracy forces must:

- Demonstrate widespread popular repudiation of the putschists' claims to legitimacy through noncooperation and disobedience;
- Prevent them from taking effective control of the political machinery of the state;
- Block the putschists' attempts to control the media and maintain popular control of communications, including print media, broadcasting, and the Internet; and
- Resist the putschists' efforts to control or neutralize independent institutions.

The guidelines they lay out for such resistance include:

- Refusing to cooperate with any putschist attempts to control the government apparatus or society;
- Maintaining nonviolent discipline in resistance activities;
- Continuing normal operations according to the constitution, laws and policies of the legitimate pre-coup government and preserving functioning political and social organizations;
- Refusing to provide information, supplies, or equipment to the putschists and their collaborators or disseminate their propaganda; and
- Documenting the putschists' repression and other illegal activities.

Richard Taylor's *Training Manual for Nonviolent Defense Against the Coup d'Etat*, originally written for a workshop in Russia in the mid-1990s before being revised, updated, and published in 2011 by Nonviolence International, is largely based on Sharp and Jenkins's theoretical model. Emphasizing the need to prepare prior to a coup, and given the narrow window of time available to successfully mobilize resistance, the manual was designed to prepare populations on the most effective and quickest means of resistance mobilization, should circumstances require it.

The Sharp and Jenkins monograph (and by extension, Taylor's manual) looks at just three cases and does not analyze the differences between the cases or compare them to cases of coup resistance that failed. It also does not look at the long-term impact of the coup resistance. While the basic assumptions and analysis they outline regarding anti-coup resistance struggles are quite valid, the ability with which pro-democracy movements can apply these principles can vary depending on the circumstances facing a particular resistance campaign.

Sharon Nepstad's 2015 textbook *Nonviolent Struggle: Theories, Strategies, and Dynamics* includes "Anti-Coup Defense" as one of the nine types of nonviolent action, summarizes Sharp and Jenkins's findings, and provides a brief account of the 1985 mobilization against the attempted coup in Argentina, but provides little new analysis.

This monograph builds on Sharp and Jenkins's original work, but offers an entirely new analytical, category-based and case study-enriched perspective on understanding how civil resistance against coups has worked. By offering additional case studies and analysis, this monograph can provide a greater understanding of how Sharp and Jenkins's principles can actually be applied.

Part 1
Six Coup Scenarios Illustrated Through 12 Case Studies

1) Post-Coup Civil Resistance that led to Coup Reversals

The first pair of cases, the Soviet Union and Thailand, Scenario 1 (see page 14), examines two countries with longstanding authoritarian traditions, which had been evolving towards greater democracy—only to be subjected to a coup by reactionary elements. However, the populations, which had previously largely accepted forcible, top-down changes in leadership, instead moved to successfully resist such changes.

Soviet Union, July 1991

After rising to power in 1985, Communist Party leader Mikhail Gorbachev—recognizing the failures of the Soviet system and the need for major reforms—promoted policies of *glasnost* (openness) and *perestroika* (restructuring). These policies allowed for greater political pluralism and the decentralization of power on a number of levels, including greater autonomy for the country's 15 constituent republics. By 1991, nonviolent campaigns for outright independence in some of these republics were gaining momentum, particularly in the Baltic nations of Estonia, Latvia, and Lithuania, the latter of which had unilaterally declared independence but was still occupied by Soviet forces.

On August 18 of that year, party hardline opponents of liberalization, fearing the collapse of the Soviet Union, detained Gorbachev at his summer retreat in the Crimea and demanded he turn over power to his vice president. When he refused, the putschists declared that they had assumed power and banned critical media, opposition political parties, and public demonstrations. Armored divisions and paratroopers were deployed throughout Moscow, other cities, and sensitive sites around the country. In the rebellious Baltic republics, troops also seized communications facilities and blockaded major ports.

The Resistance

In response, tens of thousands of people spontaneously gathered in the streets of Moscow in opposition to the coup (see Table 1 on page 26). In a widely circulated image, Russian Federation President Boris Yeltsin climbed on top of a putschist tank and denounced what he called a "rightist, reactionary, anti-constitutional coup." Declaring "all decisions

Boris Yeltsin, President of the Russian Federation at the moment of the Soviet Union's dissolution, addressing the crowd atop a tank near the Council of Ministers building on Aug. 19, 1991. Credit: Wikimedia Commons.

and instructions of this committee to be unlawful," Yeltsin called for a "universal unlimited strike" and called on Soviet citizens, including members of the armed forces, to refuse orders from the putschists. As president of what was by far the largest of the Soviet republics, he declared that afternoon that all members of the armed forces and KGB personnel within Russia were under his command, not of the putschist-controlled Soviet government.

In Moscow, thousands gathered in front of the Russian parliament building, known as the White House, to protect it from putschist attack. They erected barricades and used trolleys, buses, and cars to block the streets. Though the putschists had planned to assault the White House, the large number of mostly unarmed civilians created a sufficient deterrent to stop the attack. The putschists declared a special state of emergency in Moscow in response to "rallies, street marches, demonstrations and instances of instigation to riots," but the protests continued.

The resistance spread nationwide, with some 200,000 protesters in Leningrad (currently Saint Petersburg) and the mayor calling for "the broadest constitutional resistance" to the coup. In Kishinev, the capital of the Republic of Moldova, tens of thousands blocked streets to prevent the movement of Soviet troops. In the Baltic republics, citizens surrounded the parliament buildings and broadcast stations to protect them from Soviet forces. In Latvia and Estonia, the parliaments met in emergency session and joined Lithuania in formally declaring their independence from the Soviet Union.

Donated radio transmitters and distributed videotapes helped circulate information that was otherwise being censored. Many technicians, reporters, and other staff in the state-run media refused to repeat putschists' announcements and instead broadcast defiant speeches by Yeltsin and others resisting the coup. Protesters in Moscow and elsewhere distributed leaflets, food, and sanctuary to soldiers, and spoke and argued with them on the streets to convince them to defect or refuse orders. This resulted in large numbers of soldiers and even entire military units switching sides. Though most Russians failed to participate in the general strike Yeltsin and others called for, work stoppages did shut down some coal fields and other important industries.

Within three days, the coup had collapsed, Gorbachev returned to Moscow, and the putschists were arrested. They did not expect that level of resistance—ranging from normally compliant Soviet journalists challenging their version of events, to soldiers who refused orders to clear the streets around the Russian parliament building. The fear and cynicism that for decades had allowed a relatively small number of Communist leaders to change the government at will was over.

The Aftermath

Soon thereafter, the Communist Party of the Soviet Union, in power since the Bolshevik Revolution of 1917, was abolished. By the end of 1991, the Soviet Union was dissolved, creating 15 new independent republics, which have subsequently evolved into a mix of democracies, dictatorships and semi-autocracies. Since the early 1990s following the coup, civil insurrections in Ukraine, Georgia, the Georgian autonomous region of Abkhazia, and Kyrgyzstan have toppled autocratic governments and strengthened democratic institutions. Pro-democracy civil resistance struggles in Belarus, Azerbaijan, Armenia, and Uzbekistan have been suppressed, at times with extraordinary violence.

Russia itself has become increasingly authoritarian under the leadership of Vladimir Putin. However, despite the Soviet Union's territorial vastness and national diversity, the reversal of the 1991 coup made possible a largely peaceful—though not entirely bloodless—transition, leading to the establishment of 15 recognized nation-states after centuries of subjugation. The defeat of the coup provided an opportunity for new political openings and attempts at democratization in Russia and the newly and re-established countries. More than 70 years of Communist Party monopoly on power and centuries of autocratic control of Central Asian, Caucasian, and Eastern European nations from Moscow came to an end.

TABLE 1: SOVIET UNION, 1991	
Main CR actors	Reformist political leaders; liberal civil society elements; citizens and officials of Baltic republics
Main coup proponents	Conservative Communist Party leaders
CR strategies & tactics	Noncooperation; protests; contestation of public space
Level of planning / strategic thought	Mixed: Largely spontaneous; leadership by reformist politicians; high in Baltics
Duration of the coup	3 days
Duration of the CR	3 days
Level of nonviolent discipline	High
Size of the movement/ diversity of anti-coup movement	Hundreds of thousands, primarily in major cities and Baltic republics
Domestic allies and loyalty shifts	Liberal elements in Communist Party; Baltic governments; media
International allies/ community	Near-universal opposition to coup
Type/rank of coup leaders	Marshall of Soviet armed forces and hardline Communist leaders
How military took over/ planned to take over	Seized government buildings
Level of repression	Moderate
Mechanism of change	Forced resignation due to lack of support
Short-term results and long-term impact of CR	Abolition of ruling party; breakup of federal republic; mixed levels of democracy; autocracy; semi-autocracy in successor republics
What happened to the movement	Leaders came to power

Thailand, May 1992

Despite a pro-democracy civil insurrection in the early 1970s, which had led to some political openness and competitive elections, Thailand struggled to create a strong democratic culture and institutions. In February of 1991, a group of military leaders calling themselves the National Peace Keeping Council (NPKC) overthrew the democratically elected but infamously corrupt government of Chatchai Chunhawan. Forming a political party known as Samakki Tham, the military junta (the governing body of putschists upon seizing power) convinced large numbers of parliamentarians to join and formed a group to rewrite the constitution.

In response, a student-initiated movement calling itself the Campaign for Popular Democracy was formed. It brought together a broad cross-section of civil society ranging from academics to the poorest sectors of society. In April of 1991, they began a campaign challenging constitutional changes under the military government's consideration that would strengthen the military's role in governance. In addition to their stated opposition to the initial draft, these groups put together an alternative document known as The People's Constitution, put before the National Assembly in June that year.

Despite support for this pro-democracy initiative from four major political parties and a broad cross-section of civil society, the military government rejected the democratic constitution. In April of 1992, they named Army Commander-in-Chief General Suchinda Kraprayoon prime minister—despite previously reassuring the nation he would not be in charge of the government, and despite the fact that he was not a member of parliament, as is customary for that office.

At this point, it became apparent to the Thai public that the NPKC's seizure of power the previous year was actually a coup d'état designed to consolidate military rule.

The Resistance

This led to the launch of a major campaign by the Students Federation and the Campaign for Popular Democracy, with the stated goal "to increase public awareness of the Thai constitution practice, encourage democratic practices, and assist in coordinating activities among other NGO's with these aims" as well as "to struggle in a nonviolent way against General Suchinda's appointment using symbolic and direct action" (Callahan, 1998).

This began with a series of hunger strikes and major street protests consisting of hundreds of thousands of demonstrators (see Table 2 on page 29). On May 14, various opposition groups formed the Confederation for Democracy, which expanded the campaign from a largely middle-class effort to one including the working class and slum dwellers. By the third week of May, over a half million people had gathered in Bangkok and attempted to seize the Government House. Though the

In 2006, the Thai army orchestrated a coup that overthrew Prime Minister Thaksin Shinawatra while he was out of the country. Credit: Wikimedia Commons.

protests remained largely nonviolent, some activists responded to security force repression with projectiles, fires, and other acts of vandalism, giving the government an excuse to crack down further.

On May 19, 1992, despite a government ban on any gathering of more than 10 people, 50,000 people gathered at Ramkhanhean University and other acts of organized resistance continued. The government responded with increased repression, including shooting into crowds of unarmed protesters. This only increased the domestic and international calls for the junta to step down, however. The people boycotted government-sponsored concerts and other events. Cab drivers refused service to members of the military. People withdrew money from military-controlled banks. The campaign was joined by much of the business sector and, by May 24, the military accepted democratic amendments to the new constitution, Suchinda resigned as Prime Minister, and an elected civilian parliamentarian was appointed to that post. By the end of June, the military-controlled parliament was abolished and democratic elections took place in September.

The Aftermath

The new democratic constitution encouraged checks and balances to minimize government abuses, including independent courts, election boards, and anti-corruption agencies, and allowed for separately elected senators. For the next 14 years, Thailand remained relatively democratic. The election of a left-leaning populist party in 2001 increased political polarization in the country, with the military temporarily seizing power

TABLE 2: THAILAND, 1992	
Main CR actors	Civilian political leaders; professionals; Buddhists; pro-democracy activists
Main coup proponents	Military junta
CR strategies & tactics	Petitioning; protests; fasting; noncooperation
Level of planning / strategic thought	High
Duration of the coup	15 months
Duration of the CR	41 days
Level of nonviolent discipline	Moderate: some arson and rioting
Size of the movement/ diversity of anti-coup movement	Hundreds of thousands, throughout urban areas of the country
Domestic allies and loyalty shifts	Civil society groups
International allies/ community	Largely neutral
Type/rank of coup leaders	Military leadership
How military took over/ planned to take over	Seized government buildings and state apparatus
Level of repression	Moderate to severe
Mechanism of change	Resignation of appointed leaders; withdrawal to barracks
Short-term results and long-term impact of CR	Democratic elections and institutions for the next 14 years followed by series of military coups, civil resistance, and democratic elections; currently under military rule
What happened to the movement	Civil society groups remain active

in 2006 before turning power over to a center-right civilian coalition. Subsequent years have seen a pattern of massive street protests involving the two major political blocs to undermine the governance of the other's prime minister in power. This effectively represents the use of nonviolent action not as a broad-based movement for democracy, but as another means of waging partisan battles. While it is certainly better to have this kind of disruption rather than a civil war, it has served to perpetuate political polarization and deadlock. This has led to periodic intervention by the military, which staged another coup in May of 2014 and has remained in power ever since.

Soviet Union and Thailand: Comparison and Conclusion

Unlike most of the other cases examined in this monograph, where the government targeted by putschists was an elected democracy, the Soviet Union in 1991 was undergoing a top-down reform. Given that neither Russia nor most of the other Soviet republics had experienced democracy or large-scale civil society movements, the success in reversing the coup was all the more remarkable.

An important exception, however, was the Baltic Republics, which had enjoyed 20 years of independence between the fall of the czarist Russian Empire and World War II; had never fully accepted their incorporation into the Soviet Union; and for several years had experience large-scale civil resistance campaigns in support of independence. Indeed, the three Baltic nations' aspirations for independence served as a major motivation for the coup.

Relative to the size of the Soviet Union, the numbers of people actively involved in the protests in Russia following the coup were not as large as most of these other cases, and the call for a general strike largely went unheeded. Yet, for a country that had experienced so little organized dissent of any kind to have such public protest at all (even if limited to major cities) was apparently enough for the putschists to recognize that they would not be able to hold on to power, particularly given additional resistance from major sectors of the government, the Communist Party, and state-controlled media in what had once been a totalitarian state.

Thailand had experienced some limited if uneven political pluralism during the 18 years following the 1973 pro-democracy uprising. The military did not allow for a full democratic opening, however, and some of the intervening governments in Thailand were seen as corrupt and plutocratic. Therefore, they did not solicit the kind of enthusiasm that would normally lead to a spirited defense of civilian institutions in response to a temporary military intervention. Thais were able to mobilize effectively once it became apparent that the military was actually planning to control the government for an indefinite period. As with the Russians, then, the lack of a democratic culture and cynicism towards civilian rulers did not prevent them from putting their bodies on the line in support of greater political freedom.

There are obviously many profound differences between the political situation in the Soviet Union and Thailand at the time of these uprisings. One prominent difference, for example, was the Communist Party's overbearing monopoly of power in the Soviet Union. However, Thailand shared a history of autocratic rule with Russia and other Soviet republics. Previous purges and shifts in Communist leadership in Moscow and military takeovers in Bangkok had been taking place for decades with little response from the public. As a result, the putschists in both cases were clearly caught off-guard by the unprecedented negative responses of ordinary citizens to their efforts to seize power. The relatively smaller numbers of protesters in the Soviet case was partially compensated by greater divisions within ruling circles, yet in both cases a sufficient number of elite elements whom the putschists relied upon recognized that it was not worth the fight and the shedding of civilian blood to attempt to stay in power.

> *Putschists in the Soviet Union and Thailand were clearly caught off-guard by the unprecedented negative responses of ordinary citizens to their efforts to seize power.*

2) Preventing the Consolidation of a Coup in Progress

Among the most impressive utilization of civil resistance has been when the population has responded to attempted coups prior to the consolidation of power. In these cases, France and Argentina, Scenario 2 (see page 15), civil resistance served notice to those who were uncertain of which side to support that a military takeover of the country would not go smoothly—ultimately tipping the balance in favor of the civilian government.

France, April 1961

As of the early 1960s, France—like much of northern and western Europe—had been a democratic republic for nearly a century, save for the 1940-45 German occupation. However, the emergence of the pro-Nazi Vichy government and the ease with which German occupiers found willing collaborators during that period raised concerns over the commitment to democracy in some sectors of French society. The ultimate test came in April of 1961 when, after seven years of a bloody counter-insurgency war in Algeria against nationalists fighting for independence from France, French President Charles de Gaulle announced that his government would begin negotiations to end 130 years of French colonial rule. With nearly one million French colonists living in the country, some whose families had been there for generations, the prospects of no longer enjoying the benefits of white minority rule created a backlash from the French right, who were well-represented in the French armed forces.

On Friday night, April 21, four generals led a regiment to take over government offices in Algiers, the Algerian capital. They arrested a number of loyalist generals who led the colonial administration and announced their control of legal and civil government in the colony as well as all radio stations and newspapers. It soon became clear that neither the French government in Paris nor the putschists in Algiers were willing to compromise. It also became apparent that this was in fact an attempt to forcibly seize power not just in Algeria, but in France itself. Indeed, the putschists had developed plans, after consolidating control in Algiers and other major Algerian coastal cities where the vast majority of the French population was located, to organize a seizure of Paris. Roughly a half million French soldiers, constituting a majority of the country's armed forces, were stationed in Algeria at that point in time.

The Resistance

French President Charles de Gaulle immediately gave a nationwide address calling for popular resistance to the coup attempt. Following emergency meetings over the weekend between French political parties and trade unions, a one-hour general strike and public protests took place that Monday, April 24, 1961, to indicate a willingness to resist any efforts to threaten civilian rule in France itself (see Table 3 on page 34). Noting a likely air invasion of rebel soldiers from Algeria, Prime Minister Michel Debré called on citizens to be ready to rush to the airfields to persuade the incoming soldiers to remain loyal to civilian authorities. Hundreds of people pre-emptively went to the airfields to prepare vehicles to physically block the runways. In Algeria, French loyalists began making copies of de Gaulle's speech calling for resistance, circulating them among French soldiers and French civilians. Loyalist military pilots in Algeria flew over half of the fighter planes and transporters back to France while mysterious claims of sudden mechanical failures grounded others.

While top French officers appeared to remain neutral, the majority of ordinary soldiers—who were largely conscripts—remained in their barracks in defiance of putschists' orders to mobilize. Mid-level officers deliberately misplaced orders and documents from the putschists in support of the rebellion. Still others slowed up military communications and transportation. Within certain regiments, soldiers set up self-governing committees outside of the military command structure. Some civil servants went on strike while others hid critical documents and files.

While the French government engaged in a number of contingency plans to resist the spread of the coup to the French mainland by military means, it soon became apparent that the civil resistance actions were preventing coup-plotters from achieving their objectives. In Algeria, the police force switched sides and pledged support for the civilian government. Though de Gaulle called on loyalist troops to attack the rebels, they did not wish to participate in initiating a civil war among the French. Also recognizing their successes using nonviolent resistance, the loyalist troops did not engage in any sort of violence against the putschists. By the evening of April 25, 1961, the coup leaders abandoned their posts and fled.

The Aftermath

Algeria received its independence the following year and France has remained one of the world's leading democracies. One of the more politically polarized of European societies, a strong trade union movement and a tradition of youth-led resistance has resulted in periodic demonstrations involving millions of people nationwide and an unsuccessful proto-revolutionary uprising in May of 1968. A strong nationalist and populist far-right party has increased its following in recent years. Yet the defense of democratic institutions remains strong within left, centrist, and moderate conservative elements, collectively representing a sizeable majority of French society. At the same time, the military has remained solidly under elected civilian government control.

TABLE 3: FRANCE, 1961	
Main CR actors	Elected civilian leadership; civil society; trade unionist; lower ranks of military
Main coup proponents	Military putschists; French colonists in Algeria
CR strategies & tactics	Noncooperation; strikes
Level of planning / strategic thought	Medium
Duration of the coup	4 days
Duration of the CR	4 days
Level of nonviolent discipline	High
Size of the movement/ diversity of anti-coup movement	Millions
Domestic allies and loyalty shifts	Broad cross-section of French society
International allies/ community	Widespread opposition
Type/rank of coup leaders	Right-wing army generals
How military took over/ planned to take over	Seized military bases and government offices in Algeria
Level of repression	Minimal
Mechanism of change	Arrest of leaders
Short-term results and long-term impact of CR	Maintaining democracy and preventing potential civil war
What happened to the movement	Civil society groups remain active

Argentina, April 1987

Democracy was restored to Argentina in 1983 after a brutal period of military rule. Under the leadership of the centrist civilian government of Raúl Alfonsín, a series of investigations and prosecutions began of former military officers suspected of involvement in the "Dirty War" between 1976-83, which had resulted in the torture and murder of at least 10,000 Argentine guerrillas, trade unionists, leftists, and other suspected dissidents. By March of 1987, 51 officers had been prosecuted, 12 of whom had been sentenced (the Supreme Court had already upheld five of those sentences). As many as 450 additional human rights prosecutions were in progress, about one-third of which implicated active-duty soldiers or officers. Anxiety was growing among those who had been active participants in state-sponsored crimes against humanity.

On April 15, 1987, Major Ernesto Barreiro (a.k.a. "Cachorro," an Air Force officer and the chief torturer at the La Perla concentration camp) refused to comply with a civilian court subpoena to appear and defend himself against allegations of murder and torture. Instead, he secluded himself within the 14th Airborne Infantry Regiment camp in the city of Cordoba, where he had support from the local Commander, Lieutenant Colonel Luis Polo. One hundred thirty fellow officers and soldiers soon joined him there and together demanded amnesty for crimes committed during the Dirty War. Allied military rebels quickly established various satellite fortifications at other military bases and barracks, such as at the Campo de Mayo infantry school (which had been the scene of many human rights crimes), where Lieutenant Colonel Aldo Rico joined with 80 other officers. Another rebellion took hold of a base in the northern city of Salta.

Participants of the coup attempt were known as *Carapintadas* (painted faces) and they called the uprising "Operación Dignidad" (Operation Dignity), insisting that they were being scapegoated for following orders. The uprising had support of a much broader segment of the military than those who personally feared prosecution, however. The Alfonsín government was determined to professionalize and depoliticize the military, which for many decades had been the most powerful institution in the country. Many of the armed forces' most influential officers were upset about the prospects of civilian oversight, both in terms of their own careers as well as in their distrust of politicians. They also held a strong belief that military leaders were the best guardians of the national interest.

Though the carapintadas did not explicitly claim they were seeking to overthrow the government, this was indeed the assumption on the part of the public, as there had been literally dozens of coup attempts in Argentina since the military first toppled a civilian government in 1930. Additional cues for this assumption included the individuals involved in the armed revolt, a series of bombings targeting the judiciary, and troops' refusal to obey orders from Army Chief of Staff General Rios Erenu to suppress the rebellion.

The Argentine military was divided. Even among those not actively part of the coup, there was hesitation and unwillingness to suppress it. And the response from President Alfonsín was ambivalent. On the one hand, he mobilized loyal army units to challenge the coup plotters and insisted "no negotiations had taken place," announcing to cheering members of Congress—who had gathered for a special emergency session—that "There's nothing to negotiate... The Argentine democracy is not negotiable" (Fitch, 2015). At the same time, Alfonsín strategically sought a compromise for "all the major political parties" to endorse. In an attempt to strike a conciliatory tone toward the rebel officers, he called them "heroes of the Malvinas war" during a public address. But the crowd found Alfonsín's gesture unnecessary and responded with "jeers and catcalls" (wsws.org, 2013).

The Resistance

As the president's office was negotiating a compromise, Argentines themselves were taking matters into their own hands. On April 17, 1987, about 500 civilians—ignoring officials' pleas to avoid the area—gathered outside the Cordoba base shouting "Long live democracy! Argentina! Argentina!" The coup plotters positioned a tank to intimidate the crowd, but the protesters marched into the base, forcing the 80 rebellious officers to surrender (Drosdoff, 1987a). Meanwhile, 400,000 people took to the streets in Buenos Aires to rally in opposition to the coup, and thousands besieged the rebel stronghold of Campo de Mayo just outside the city (see Table 4 on page 38).

Massive demonstrations took place throughout Argentina on successive days, with the rallying cry "nunca más" ("never again") in reference to a return to military rule. Throughout the country, motorists honked their horns and waved the country's flag out of their windows. The trade union federation called for a general strike, shutting down the country and enabling workers to mobilize in opposition to the coup attempt. Street art with slogans such as "for democracy—against coups" sprouted around the country (Chaffee, 1993, 126).

President Alfonsín, who had largely been in the background during this period, then became more pro-active, encouraging mass actions and lining up leaders of every major political party, along with leaders of civic organizations, business groups, the Catholic Church, and labor unions to sign a document pledging to "support in all ways possible the constitution, the normal development of the institutions of government and democracy as the only viable way of life of the Argentines." This was the first time in history that such a broad spectrum of Argentines had united in support for democracy over military rule. Empowered with such widespread support, and the coup plotters finding virtually the entire society opposed to their rebellion, President Alfonsín personally went to Campo de Mayo on April 17 and negotiated their surrender.

Raúl Alfonsín announces the end of the mutiny.
Credit: Wikimedia Commons.

This was a dramatic break in Argentina's traditional apathy and fatalism towards successive military takeovers of the government. President Alfonsín triumphantly announced, "The time of the coups has ended." A UPI wire service report at the time noted, "The message to the rebels was clear: they could hold a military base, but could not win control of the country," noting how Argentines had learned "if they stand up and be counted, a coup d'état can be avoided after all" (Drosdoff, 1987b).

The Aftermath

Argentina has remained democratic ever since. The tradition of mass nonviolent action remains, as large-scale civil resistance toppled a series of governments in late 2001 and early 2002 for ceding to international financial institutions' demands to adopt draconian austerity measures. Meanwhile, workers have seized scores of factories facing closure that are now run as worker-owned cooperatives. Other grassroots nonviolent movements have remained an important force in Argentine politics. A series of competitive democratic elections have subsequently brought both center-left and center-right governments to power. For the first time in the country's two centuries of independence, there is no longer a realistic threat of a military coup.

TABLE 4: ARGENTINA, 1987	
Main CR actors	Elected civilian leadership; civil society; trade unionists
Main coup proponents	Military putschists
CR strategies & tactics	Noncooperation; blockades; street protests; strikes
Level of planning / strategic thought	Moderate
Duration of the coup	3 days
Duration of the CR	3 days
Level of nonviolent discipline	High
Size of the movement/ diversity of anti-coup movement	Millions, primarily in capital
Domestic allies and loyalty shifts	Broad cross-section of Argentine society
International allies/ community	Widespread opposition
Type/rank of coup leaders	Right-wing army generals
How military took over/ planned to take over	Seized military bases
Level of repression	Minimal
Mechanism of change	Arrest of leaders
Short-term results and long-term impact of CR	Maintaining democracy
What happened to the movement	Civil society groups remain active

France and Argentina: Comparison and Conclusion

The success of these rather spontaneous pro-democracy campaigns was all the more remarkable since the resistance had to mobilize almost immediately, given that the coups were in progress and there was little time to develop a strategy. In both cases, key sectors of the military appeared to be neutral—an indication that they were not willing to defend democracy on principle and likely would have supported the coup if it had looked more promising. What the civil resistance accomplished was leading hesitant military units to conclude that the costs of a coup would be too high—in terms of the numbers of unarmed civilians they would likely have to kill, the prominent individuals they would have to arrest, and the soldiers and civil servants on whose obedience they could not rely. Without the civil resistance, these likely costs would not have been apparent.

> *A clear message that military rule would be met by massive noncooperation was enough to tilt the balance of power against a successful coup.*

The success of the Argentine case is all the more remarkable given how that country's weak democratic tradition and history of paternalistic politics contrasts sharply with France's revolutionary tradition. However, both countries had strong trade union movements, and the recent experiences of Nazi/Vichy rule in France and military dictatorships in Argentina gave peoples in both countries a strong incentive to resist returning to autocratic rule.

One key difference was that the Argentine president appeared ready to compromise while the French president was willing to use military force. In both cases, however, it was the emergence of a civil resistance campaign against the coups that made both of these potentially dangerous alternatives unnecessary. Another key difference between these two cases was that in Argentina the coup attempt was centered near the capital, while the case in France was localized in a faraway colonial possession. In the former case, pro-democracy forces had to mobilize in larger numbers, and more directly, to provide an adequate deterrence to putschists moving forward. In both cases, however, a clear message that military rule would be met by massive noncooperation was enough to tilt the balance of power against a successful coup.

3) Defending Newly-won Democracy against a Coup

The following two cases, Bolivia and Burkina Faso, Scenario 3 (see page 15), involve countries in which a longstanding authoritarian government had recently been ousted through civil resistance and a new democratic government has come to power. Reactionary forces within the military then attempt to turn the clock back by staging a coup to reinstate authoritarian rule, but their efforts are soon reversed in a new wave of civil resistance that ousts the newly formed regime and restores democracy.

Bolivia, November 1978

In 1978, a protracted nonviolent struggle against the dictatorship of General Hugo Banzer, who had initially been installed in a U.S.-backed coup in 1971, forced the military leader's resignation. The elections of July 1979 ended in a virtual tie between Hernán Siles Zuazo and Victor Paz Estensorro, two former colleagues from the National Revolutionary Movement (MNR), which held power during the dozen years after Bolivia's 1952 revolution. Zuazo was a member of the leftist Unidad Democrática y Popular (UDP), while Estensorro was still running for election under the MNR banner. Congress broke the stalemate by electing the center-left Senate leader Walter Guevara, another prominent figure who had served with the MNR government, as president the following month. The initial return to civilian rule was short-lived, however, as a certain General Alberto Natusch Busch seized power in a coup on November 1.

The Resistance

That night, thousands of Bolivians took to the streets of the capital of La Paz in protest, with hundreds erecting barricades to protect working-class neighborhoods, challenging tanks with nothing more than their bodies and cobblestones. A general strike—the first in nearly a decade—was declared as hundreds of thousands of Bolivians began marching on La Paz (see Table 5 on page 43). Meanwhile, mostly youthful demonstrators rallied outside the parliament building to protect it from an anticipated military assault. When the legislature condemned the coup and pledged not to cooperate with the de facto regime, Natusch Busch declared the Congress illegal. He then attempted to placate the growing uprising by offering reforms and pay raises, but the protesters demanded nothing less than the restoration of democracy.

Unable to mollify the opposition, his troops went on the offensive, blowing up most of the headquarters of the Central Obrera Boliviana (Bolivian Workers Central, the trade union federation known by the Spanish acronym COB), shooting up the working-class neighborhood where the resistance was centered from a helicopter rented from a U.S. company, and moving armored vehicles to challenge the "moral barricades" of the pro-democracy demonstrators. Over 300 activists were killed during the regime's first two weeks—more than during the entire seven years of the Banzer dictatorship.

Still feeling pressure, Natusch Busch attempted to compromise by proposing to establish a tripartite regime consisting of himself, representatives from Congress, and the COB. While some of the leading political parties appeared willing to consider such an arrangement, the COB rejected any concessions short of the general's resignation. Passive noncooperation by the police increased and, despite generous bonuses, key elements of the armed forces became less and less reliable. Even in the face of the repression, by the end of the regime's second week in power, more than 600,000 people had descended on La Paz, a larger number than the entire population of the capital at that time.

At the beginning of the third week of the coup, COB leaders entered the presidential palace to personally confront Natusch Busch in his office, demanding that he reveal his political program. With the country shut down by a general strike and his own palace besieged by pro-democracy activists, Natusch Busch, recognizing his limited options at that point, felt compelled to respond to labor leaders that his political program would be "yours!" The COB leaders, however, rejected the offer of adopting their program under military rule. Instead, they insisted on a return to democracy—starting with Natusch Busch resign and allow a return to democracy. He stepped down the following day, after only 16 days in office.

The Aftermath

The restored Congress then elected the president of Chamber of Deputies, Lidia Gueiler, as the country's president. New elections were called for July of 1980, leading to a solid victory for the leftist UDP coalition. Before they could take office however, another coup took place, bringing in the most repressive dictatorship of this period,

led by General Luis García Meza. Being better organized and more systematic in their repression, these putschists were able to prevent another coup reversal like the one that had toppled Natusch Busch. However, popular pressure led to Garcia Meza stepping down a year later and democracy being fully restored in October of 1982.

Bolivian politics in subsequent years has not been smooth, even with the return of democracy. Large-scale nonviolent resistance movements have continued, particularly in support of indigenous rights and in opposition to neoliberal economic policies and government overreach. It was also out of this growth in massive nonviolent movements in Bolivia, particularly within the indigenous community, that the presidential campaign of Evo Morales emerged.

Morales not only became the first indigenous president of this majority-Indian nation, but also the first president who emerged from neither the military nor established political parties. His government has engaged in radical social reforms which have improved the lives of millions of poor Bolivians but have polarized the country. Morales has been challenged by two main groups: right-wing separatists in the Mezza Luna region in the eastern part of the country, and by those on his left pressuring him through frequent, disruptive but largely nonviolent protests to more fully live up to his socialist rhetoric. Despite these pressures, the country has largely been able to maintain its democratic structure and institutions.

TABLE 5: BOLIVIA, 1978	
Main CR actors	Pro-democracy activists; trade unionists; urban working class; civilian politicians
Main coup proponents	Military junta
CR strategies & tactics	Noncooperation; protests; strikes; contestation of public space
Level of planning / strategic thought	High: re-mobilization of forces from recent pro-democracy struggle
Duration of the coup	16 days
Duration of the CR	16 days
Level of nonviolent discipline	Moderate; some rioting
Size of the movement/ diversity of anti-coup movement	Close to 1 million, nearly one-fifth of the population, including indigenous and mestizo
Domestic allies and loyalty shifts	Broad cross-section of Bolivian society
International allies/ community	Largely neutral
Type/rank of coup leaders	Army general
How military took over/ planned to take over	Seized government buildings; attacking opposition strongholds
Level of repression	Moderate to severe
Mechanism of change	Forced resignation due to mass noncooperation
Short-term results and long-term impact of CR	Restoration of democracy for 21 months, followed by a successful coup, which was eventually brought down three years later; subsequent democracy
What happened to the movement	Remained strong; challenged by a more serious coup two years later

Burkina Faso, September 2015

In 2014, this impoverished, landlocked country in West Africa had been ruled by President Blaise Compaoré since he overthrew and executed the country's popular leftist leader Thomas Sankara 27 years earlier. When he tried to extend his rule even longer through a proposed change in the Constitution, massive protests erupted nationwide on October 28, 2014, forcing Compaoré's resignation three days later. Lieutenant Colonel Isaac Zida became interim leader, but opposition parties, civil society groups, and religious leaders successfully pushed for a civilian-led transitional authority to dismantle the dictatorship's legacies and oversee elections the following year. As a result, veteran diplomat Michel Kafando became the acting president and Zida was named acting prime minister and defense minister.

Women marching for democracy, spatula in hand, during October 2014 protests. Credit: *Observatoire du Genre.*

Among the policies implemented to marginalize anti-democratic elements was the decision to bar anyone who had supported Compaoré's efforts to extend his term from taking part in the election, scheduled for October of 2015. This angered some still-influential military officers allied with the former dictator, including those in the Regiment of Presidential Security (RSP), which effectively served as Compaoré's personal army and was under increasing scrutiny. Indeed, a commission appointed by the new civilian government noted in a report released in early September that year that the RSP had become "an army within an army" and called for it to be dismantled and its members redeployed elsewhere in the armed forces (Bonkoungou and Bavier, 2015a).

On September 16, 2015, RSP members seized government buildings in the capital of Ouagadougou, detaining President Kafando, Prime Minister Zida, and several cabinet members. The following day, the coup leaders announced the dismissal of Kafando, the dissolution of the government and the transitional legislature, and the establishment of what they paradoxically called the National Council for Democracy (*Conseil national pour la Démocratie*, or CND) which they claimed would oversee eventual elections under the leadership of General Gilbert Diendéré.

The Resistance

A grassroots left-leaning movement known as Le Balai Citoyen, (literally meaning "the citizens' broom" or a citizen-led movement for sweeping change), which had played a major role in the 2014 uprising, immediately called upon the people of Ouagadougou to gather in Revolution Square outside the presidential palace to protest the coup (*Le Monde Afrique*). As hundreds of protesters assembled, shouting "Down with the RSP!" and "We want elections!", soldiers fired warning shots and began beating protesters when they failed to disperse. The putschists shut down several private radio stations covering the protests (Flynn, 2015), yet news of resistance, including calls for strikes and demonstrations from trade unions and political parties, was circulated through social networks and clandestine radio stations. Unable to gather in a central location—such as the Place de la Nation, the site of the major pro-democracy rallies the previous year—demonstrators spread out for smaller protests in various neighborhoods (see Table 6 on page 48).

Le Balai Citoyen headquarters in Ouagadougou, Burkina Faso. Credit: Amber French.

Outside the capital, resistance was even stronger. Ignoring curfew orders, residents of the second-largest city Bobo Dioulasso continued in all-night protests. Other major cities in each region (Fada N'Gourma in the east, Banfora in the southwest, Dori and Ouahigouya in the north, and Koudougou in the center) took to the streets, marching to their respective main squares, protesting in front of military camps, and constructing barricades of stones and burning tires. Protesters were diverse in terms of class and ethnicity, largely representative of the urban population as a whole. Women played a prominent role, emerging from their homes, waving spatulas in the air—a rare sign of disapproval in Burkinabé culture which signaled to others across the country the degree of seriousness the resistance was reaching. While neither police nor the military joined the protesters, they generally did not try to suppress them. In addition, shopkeepers and professionals stayed home from work as part of a general strike (Bertrand, 2015).

International reaction to the coup was uniformly negative. On September 18, the African Union suspended Burkina Faso's membership and placed sanctions on coup leaders (Ouedraogo, 2015a). Senegalese president Macky Sall, who also served as Chairman of the Economic Community of West African States (ECOWAS), traveled to Ouagadougou to hold talks with Diendéré, along with Benin president Boni Yayi (Hien, 2015).

During the third day of talks, coup supporters, in an apparent effort to intimidate the visiting presidents, violently stormed into the lobby of the hotel where the talks were taking place, but the leaders of the neighboring countries persisted. Hours later, a draft agreement was announced which, while releasing the captive government leaders and formally restoring Kafando as president, gave into key CND demands. These included allowing excluded candidates to participate in the election, providing amnesty for coup participants, delaying the scheduled election (Fort and Hein, 2015a), and allowing Diendéré to continue in his post during the remainder of the transitional period (Ouedraogo, 2015b).

While some West African leaders appeared willing to compromise, the people of Burkina Faso apparently felt otherwise. Pro-democracy activists, arguing that the proposed terms offered too many concessions to the coup leaders, continued their protests and the draft agreement was never implemented. It soon was apparent that the putschists never controlled much of the country beyond Ouagadougou and protests continued even in the capital. On September 21, 2015, army leaders announced that loyalist soldiers were marching towards the capital to challenge the coup. In Koudougou, the country's third largest city located 100 miles west of Ouagadougou, people cheered soldiers passing through on their way to challenge the putschists (Taoko, 2015).

As a conciliatory gesture, Diendéré announced he would release Prime Minister Zida (Bonkoungou and Coulibaly, 2015a) and agreed to allow Kafando to be restored to power as president under certain conditions. But Zida resisted surrendering, saying he wanted "to continue the discussions" and was "ready to implement ECOWAS' decisions" (Jullian, 2015). After initially rejecting demands for surrender, the RSP agreed on the afternoon of the 22nd to withdraw to its barracks in return for not being attacked and for the regular army withdrawing from Ouagadougou. Kafando was reinstalled as president the following day at a ceremony in the presence of ECOWAS leaders, and Zida returned to his post as prime minister.

When the cabinet met for the first time following the coup attempt on September

25, they dismissed the Minister of Security and abolished the RSP, as well as the position of head of the president's military council. When Diendéré and the RSP, confined to their base in the Ouaga 2000 neighborhood of the capital, refused to surrender their arms, the facility was forcibly seized by the army with very little resistance. Diendéré and other RSP leaders responsible for the coup were arrested, tried, and imprisoned. Lower-ranking RSP members were reassigned to other military units. In the course of the week-long coup, 11 people were killed and more than 250 were injured, but democracy was restored.

The Aftermath

On November 29, 2015, in simultaneous presidential and legislative elections with a 60% turnout, Roch Marc Kaboré of the Movement of People for Progress (MPP) was elected president. Burkina Faso has continued to function as a democratic republic ever since with an active civil society engaged in further consolidating democratic gains.

The successful 2014 pro-democracy uprising and this 2015 reversal of the coup together have been seen as a very significant democratic transition for West Africa and a demonstration that military coups on the continent can be reversed in the face of sustained resistance. While opposition to the coup from the regular armed forces and neighboring countries were important factors in the coup's failure, the popular resistance played perhaps the most critical role, particularly in blocking the initial compromise agreement which granted concessions to the putschists. When Diendéré stepped down as interim leader on September 23, he acknowledged that the coup was a mistake, noting that "we knew the people were not in favor of it. That is why we have given up" (Fort and Hien, 2015b).

TABLE 6: BURKINA FASO, 2015

Main CR actors	Pro-democracy activists; civilian politicians; some military
Main coup proponents	Military junta; leaders of former ruling party
CR strategies & tactics	Protests; blockades; strikes; noncooperation
Level of planning / strategic thought	Moderate; re-mobilization of forces from recent pro-democracy struggles
Duration of the coup	7 days
Duration of the CR	7 days
Level of nonviolent discipline	High, through loyal army units utilized to arrest putschists
Size of the movement/ diversity of anti-coup movement	Hundreds of thousands; throughout urban areas of the country
Domestic allies and loyalty shifts	Civil society groups; trade unions; most politicians; some segments of military
International allies/ community	Largely negative; opposition led by regional organization
Type/rank of coup leaders	General of presidential guards
How military took over/ planned to take over	Seized government buildings; held leading officials hostage
Level of repression	Moderate to severe
Mechanism of change	Withdrew to barracks; later arrested
Short-term results and long-term impact of CR	Democratic elections and institutions still in place
What happened to the movement	Civil society groups remain active

Bolivia and Burkina Faso: Comparison and Conclusion

Given how reactionary forces allied with the old regime will often plot to take control of the country yet again, these two cases serve as reminders of the importance of pro-democracy forces remaining vigilant, politically engaged, and willing to take to the streets again to defend their gains. Though both countries were extremely poor and ethnically diverse, Bolivia had a much stronger trade union movement, well-established political parties, an activist wing of the Catholic Church, and a longer history of civil resistance. However, in both cases, the protracted struggles in the preceding years that eventually led to the ouster of the previous dictatorships resulted in a degree of conscientization and empowerment in a population which—like those in most neighboring countries—had suffered under decades of dictatorship. As a result, the Bolivians and Burkinabés shed their sense of fatalism which had until then let violent seizures of power go virtually unchallenged.

> *Having tasted freedom, there was a popular determination not to let the country go back to its former autocratic rule.*

Now, many of the networks and other tools for mobilization that arose during the earlier struggles could be easily reactivated in the event of another coup attempt—rather than movements having to start from scratch. This is a particularly important asset when a quick response is so essential. Many movement participants felt that sacrifices made during the initial struggle should not be wasted by such a quick reversal of the gains made. Having tasted freedom, there was a popular determination not to let the country go back to its former autocratic rule.

4) Coups Allegedly in Defense of Democracy

The next two sets of cases, Venezuela and Mali, Scenario 4 (see page 15), involve situations where the military—in response to large-scale civil insurrections—ousts an authoritarian or semi-authoritarian leader. In some cases, these more resemble a coup de grace than a coup d'état, since the incumbent autocrat had clearly lost support of the population and his orders were no longer being consistently followed.

This first pairing, Venezuela (1958) and Mali (1991), involves cases where democratic forces were able to consolidate power following the coup.

Venezuela, January 1958

In January 1958, Venezuela had been under a military dictatorship since the overthrow of the democratically elected government led by the center-left Acción Democrática (Democratic Action Party, or AD) a decade earlier. With the assassination of coup leader Colonel Delgado Chalbaud in 1950, General Marcos Pérez Jiménez achieved de facto control, officially gaining the title of president two years later. A technocratic authoritarian, Jiménez restructured and modernized the Venezuelan armed forces to assure their loyalty, including making efforts to separate the officer corps from civilian society (Trinkunas, 2005, 67-68).

Despite the technocratic pretenses of the government, the regime was characterized by crony capitalism that won allies among conservative civilian elites but began to alienate some junior officers. The Venezuelan military had also been experiencing divisions since the coup, with the majority solidly behind Jiménez. Nevertheless, a strong minority was open to the possibility of limited civilian rule. As dissent also grew within the civilian population, Jiménez established a new police force within the Interior Ministry called the Seguridad Nacional (National Security Force), which eventually wielded more power than the regular armed forces.

The Resistance

Despite the repression and corruption, rapid economic growth and impressive development projects initially limited dissent. By most appearances, Jiménez appeared to be firmly in control. Opposition parties were banned and most leading opposition figures either went into exile or were jailed. Jiménez also enjoyed the strong support of the United States, the hegemonic power in the hemisphere. Small-scale acts of armed resistance by the Venezuelan Communist Party were easily crushed.

Despite this, civil society grew dramatically during this period, and clandestine opposition movements had begun to emerge by late 1956 (see Table 7 on page 54). In addition, women formed organizations and became active in the resistance, taking advantage of the greater political space they had relative to men (in large part because the dictatorship did not take them seriously). Posing as wives, mothers, or sisters, they were able to share messages between jailed opposition leaders and the underground resistance (Galván, 2013, 68-69). The Catholic hierarchy, which had been generally friendly with the government, began to distance itself in face of growing repression as Monseñor Rafael Arias Blanco, the archbishop of Caracas, denounced the violence of the government (Scheina, 2003, 230).

Popular discontent greatly increased when the country was hit by a recession in the fall of 1957, as a result of a drop in oil prices. The first major street protests took place when, instead of holding competitive elections as promised when Jiménez's five-year term expired, the regime announced a plebiscite on whether or not he should be allowed to remain in power for an additional five years. The December 15 vote was discernably fraudulent, as the regime claimed victory with an 85% in favor within two hours of the closing of the polls.

> *Women became key actors and communicators in the resistance, much to the surprise of the dictatorship, which largely ignored women as potential threats to their grip on power.*

A poorly organized coup attempt on January 1, 1958 was defeated, revealing divisions in the armed forces that emboldened the growing civilian opposition. On January 9, the underground opposition known as Junta Patriótica engaged in civil disobedience and street actions. Tens of thousands poured out onto the streets, particularly in the poorer neighborhoods of the capital Caracas, shouting "Down with the chains!" (Da Silva, 2013, 59). The government cracked down harshly, even closing the country's high schools and universities to suppress student protests. Professional organizations representing doctors, lawyers, engineers and professors began organizing, and trade unions mobilized. Various national institutions which had until then largely been silent—including the College of Engineering, the Venezuelan Association of Journalists, and prominent business organizations—issued manifestoes against the regime.

On January 13, Acción Democrática, the largest opposition party, joined the Junta Patriótica and encouraged its members to join the protest. Though largely nonviolent, rioting, raids on government buildings, and attacks on security forces took place, including some exchanges of gunfire. An estimated 300 protesters were killed in the course of the insurrection.

A general strike was called for January 21, resulting in a virtual paralysis of all social and economic activity in the country. Most businesses closed voluntarily, though others were forced to close by protesters. The following day, naval units in Puerto Cabello, located about 200 kilometers west of Caracas, rebelled. Jiménez ordered the nearby Valencia army garrison to attack the rebellious seamen, but the commander refused.

Meanwhile, several destroyers with marine detachments began sailing towards La Guaira, the port just north of the capital. The dictator then ordered an army unit based in Caracas to attack La Guaira, but the commander instead stationed his forces in the hills between the port and the capital to protect the navy. In Caracas itself, cadets at the military academy revolted and were surrounded by troops from the Bolivar Battalion, but they refused to fire. Jiménez then tried to negotiate with the rebellious army and navy units, but they refused to compromise, instead demanding his departure. He fled to the Dominican Republic early on the morning of January 23 (Trinkunas, 60-61).

A Provisional Government Junta was established under the leadership of a Governing Board to oversee the restoration of democracy, consisting of Admiral Wolfgang Larrazábal as its chairman, along with four Army colonels. Protests of military domination continued, and military officers were soon replaced by prominent businessmen and other representatives of independent sectors, with journalist Fabricio Ojeda becoming chair. Democratic elections were held by the end of the year, resulting in a victory for the AD presidential nominee Rómulo Betancourt.

The Aftermath

Venezuela's three main parties—the AD, COPEI (Social Christian Party), and Unión Republicana Democrática (URD)—signed the Puntofijo Pact which guaranteed power sharing and the maintaining of democratic institutions. During subsequent decades, Venezuela remained South America's most stable democracy as much of the rest of the continent suffered under right-wing military dictatorships. However, the pact resulted in exclusionary politics and increasingly corrupt plutocratic rule, with growing social and economic inequality, compounded by a boom and bust cycle from the country's oil-based economy.

The 1998 election of left-wing populist Hugo Chavez, a former lieutenant colonel who had led an unsuccessful coup in 1992, ushered in a period of radical social and economic reform and increasingly polarized politics. While re-elected three times in what were generally seen as free and fair elections, increasing state power and suppression of civil liberties, combined with economic mismanagement and corruption, led to growing dissent. He remained popular, however, particularly among the country's poor.

While engaging in various forms of nonviolent resistance, the elite-led opposition initially attracted little support beyond the more privileged segments of society. A right-wing coup in 2002 was reversed in just four days as a result of popular protests and divisions within the security forces. Upon his death in 2013, Chavez was succeeded by his vice president Nicolás Maduro, who increased political repression and the state's authoritarian reach. In response to these developments, civil resistance led by the growing and increasingly diverse opposition has grown dramatically, as has government repression.

Interestingly, both the Venezuelan government and the opposition celebrate and claim the legacy of the 1958 pro-democracy uprising. Armed communist guerrilla movements emerged in the 1960s, but never gained much traction. Even though policy choices were driven through a process of elite bargaining, civil society groups continued to grow, exercising their influence on the local level, and helping the country maintain democracy while most of the continent suffered under dictatorship.

TABLE 7: VENEZUELA, 1958	
Main CR actors	Civil society organizations
Main coup proponents	Military dictatorship
CR strategies & tactics	Protests; general strike; confronting security forces
Level of planning / strategic thought	Moderate; underground organizations; calls for general strike
Duration of the coup	11 months
Duration of the CR	3 weeks
Level of nonviolent discipline	Moderate; some rioting; attacking security forces
Size of the movement/ diversity of anti-coup movement	Hundreds of thousands; throughout urban areas of the country
Domestic allies and loyalty shifts	Opposition political parties; professionals; Catholic Church; unions; some segments of military
International allies/ community	Neutral
Type/rank of coup leaders	General and commander of armed forces
How military took over/ planned to take over	Refusal to suppress uprising; demanding president's departure
Level of repression	Severe prior to coup; dramatically reduced thereafter
Mechanism of change	Deposed dictator
Short-term results and long-term impact of CR	Democratic elections and institutions developed
What happened to the movement	Civil society organizations remained, though political involvement decreased

Mali, March 1991

The Republic of Mali is an impoverished landlocked country in the Sahel region of northwestern Africa. Several clandestine parties emerged after Moussa Traoré in 1968 led a military coup d'état to overthrew the left-leaning nationalist government in place since independence from France eight years prior. These parties were underground until 1990 when, in response to international criticism, the Traoré regime legalized an association consisting of the National Democratic Initiative Committee and others, which united to form the Alliance for Democracy in Mali (ADEMA).

ADEMA's historical roots and their proven ability to stay strong and united against persecution lent them legitimacy in the eyes of many Malians. Several different clandestine organizations came together under the persecution of the military regime, but it was ADEMA's original organizational structure, characterized by its decentralization, that maintained its strength. The organization itself functioned in a manner consistent with democratic principles. This gave it legitimacy as a leader of the resistance movement for democracy. It also served as a framework for its subsequent transformation into a political party.

In the years leading up to the overthrow of the dictatorial regime, ADEMA was able to organize unions and student groups to create a unified front. In March of 1991, ADEMA was one of the main proponents and planners of a series of demonstrations, protests and strikes throughout the country. ADEMA broadened its geographical influence by unifying many organizations whose histories go back as far as 1968. Also, because of ADEMA's longevity, many of its members were well-educated, middle-aged teachers and health professionals. Their skills and experience in the public sphere helped bring ADEMA's message to rural communities throughout the country, as well as recruit members and raise funds for the democratic movement. ADEMA's supporters also consisted of *griots*, hereditary musicians who spread the historical roots of democracy in Mali to the largely illiterate rural population.

The Resistance

Peaceful student protests in January of 1991 were brutally suppressed, with mass arrests and torture of leaders and participants. Scattered acts of rioting and vandalism of public buildings followed, but most dissident actions remained nonviolent (see Table 8 on page 59). From March 22 to March 26, 1991, urban and rural communities alike held mass pro-democracy rallies and a nationwide strike, which collectively became known as *les événements* ("the events") or "the March Revolution."

In the capital of Bamako, soldiers opened fire indiscriminately on large crowds of nonviolent demonstrators which included university students and, later, trade unionists and others. Although the demonstrations were conceived of as nonviolent and nonviolent discipline had been maintained up to that point, riots broke out briefly following the shootings. Protesters erected barricades and roadblocks to protect themselves from soldiers. Traoré declared a state of emergency and imposed a nightly curfew. Despite an estimated loss of 300 lives over the course of four days, nonviolent protesters continued to come back each day to demand the resignation of the dictatorial president and the implementation of democracy.

Soldiers increasingly refused to fire into the largely nonviolent protesting crowds, and by March 26, a full-scale mutiny was in order: thousands of soldiers put down their arms and joined the pro-democracy movement. That afternoon, Lieutenant Colonel Amadou Toumani Touré, head of Traoré's presidential guard, announced on the radio that he had arrested the dictatorial president. Touré then suspended the existing institutions and took the lead in the transitional government, which was initially named the National Council of Reconciliation and later the Transitional Committee for the Welfare of the People. He appointed a civilian prime minister and promised he would neither run for president nor take over power once a president was elected in free and fair elections. He presided over a two-week national conference during the summer of 1991 which drew up a new democratic constitution and scheduled elections the following year.

The Aftermath

Meanwhile, ADEMA had become an official political party. Because of their long history of organizing, ADEMA was able to quickly evolve from a resistance movement into a representative political party. The leader of ADEMA, Alpha Oumar Konaré was the party's candidate for president. In the April 1992 elections, Konaré became president and Amadou Toumani Touré stepped down from his position as head of the transitional government. ADEMA finished first in all five regional elections.

Though like most countries in the region Mali subsequently struggled with corruption, poverty, and a weak infrastructure, it was widely considered for a time to be the most democratic country in West Africa. In 1993, the government implemented a program called the "Decentralization Mission" designed to educate and promote the rights and duties of its citizens—and ultimately to encourage popular participation in local and regional elections. Independent radio stations and newspapers emerged and the country experienced lively and open political debate.

During the 1990s, in response to Mali's international debt, international financial institutions imposed structural adjustment programs. The resulting periods of student-led protests throughout the decade against the resulting economic hardships precipitated the fall of one government through a "no confidence" vote in parliament. The tradition of nonviolent resistance against authoritarianism came to the fore in 2001, when a proposed constitutional referendum put forward by President Konaré, which would have weakened checks on presidential power, was called off after a series of pro-democracy protests. Additional peaceful protests of neo-liberal economic policies erupted in 2005.

Like a number of neighboring states, Mali's borders were drawn rather arbitrarily by colonial authorities. The result has been periodic ethnic minority rebellions, particularly the Tuaregs in the north. Soon after the March Revolution of 1991, the Malian government negotiated a peace agreement with armed Tuareg rebels in which they agreed to end their rebellion in return for a degree of autonomy. In March of 1996, a massive ceremonial burning of the rebels' surrendered weapons took place in the capital of Bamako.

This changed, however, in 2011, when the initially nonviolent uprising in Libya against the Gaddafi regime turned to armed struggle, resulting in even greater government repression and prompting NATO intervention. In the process, disparate armed groups—including Tuareg tribesmen—ended up liberating major stores of armaments. These groups passed on vast caches of weapons to Tuaregs in Mali who, now having the means to effectively challenge the Malian government militarily, dramatically escalated their long-dormant rebellion under the leadership of the National Movement for the Liberation of Azawad (MNLA).

Due to the Touré government's corruption and ineptitude as well as concerns that responding too harshly might create a backlash among the northern tribesmen, elements of the military became resentful of what they saw as inadequate support for their struggle against the Tuaregs. On March 22, 2012, U.S.-trained Army Captain Amadou Sanogo and other officers staged a coup and called for Western military intervention along the lines of Afghanistan and the "war on terror."

At the same time that the coup was causing divisions in the army, supporters of the ousted democratically elected government were amassing to protest in the capital. Taking advantage of the chaos in the south, Tuaregs quickly consolidated their hold on the northern part of the country, declaring an independent state. Then, with the Malian army routed and Tuareg forces stretched thin, radical Islamist groups—also flushed with new arms resulting from the Libya war—seized most of the towns and cities in the north before being driven back by French military intervention. The Malian military gradually allowed for the return of civilian rule which, despite ongoing threats of violence by Islamist extremists and other problems, has restored many if not all of the democratic gains it made in 1991.

TABLE 8: MALI, 1991	
Main CR actors	Major opposition party; students
Main coup proponents	Military dictatorship
CR strategies & tactics	Protests; rallies; general strike
Level of planning / strategic thought	Moderate: decentralized clandestine organizations; consciousness-raising
Duration of the coup	13 months
Duration of the CR	5 days
Level of nonviolent discipline	Relatively high despite massacres, though some rioting
Size of the movement/ diversity of anti-coup movement	Hundreds of thousands; throughout urban areas of the country
Domestic allies and loyalty shifts	Young professionals; trade unions; some segments of military
International allies/ community	Neutral
Type/rank of coup leaders	Lieutenant colonel
How military took over/ planned to take over	Seized government buildings
Level of repression	Severe prior to coup; minimal thereafter
Mechanism of change	Deposed and jailed dictator
Short-term results and long-term impact of CR	Democratic elections and institutions remained strong until 2012; more mixed subsequently
What happened to the movement	Key leaders came to power; civil society groups remain active

Venezuela and Mali: Comparison and Conclusion

The two cases in which the military oversaw a transition to democracy in the face of a popular uprising might initially appear surprising, given that neither country had had much of a history of democracy. Traoré's military coup in Mali had lasted 23 years and he appeared to have the solid support of his military.

Having already killed an estimated 300 protesters during three days of demonstrations, soldiers began refusing orders, indicating the extent of the popular resistance. It was at this moment that the commander of Traoré's own presidential guard overthrew him.

Coup leader Touré's willingness to immediately begin a democratic transition and allow for civilian leadership appears to have been the result of having calculated that two factors would have made it impossible for him to remain in power. The first was the presence of a broad alliance of democratic organizations that led the revolt. The second was the relative weakness of the military, whose status had declined under Traoré's dictatorial rule.

As for Venezuela, the military's willingness to hand over power to civilians was equally surprising, given the paucity of democratic traditions in that country. The civilian government overthrown in 1948 was Venezuela's first democratically elected government. However, as with the case of Sudan, examined below, they may have had little choice, given that the mobilized masses that had risen up against the dictator were clearly willing to continue their protests had the military done otherwise.

The differences between the two cases are striking: While Venezuela's population in 1958 was roughly the same as Mali's in 1989, the oil-rich South American nation was one of the wealthier countries in the Global South and had a relatively well-educated population. Mali was far less developed economically and suffered from high rates of illiteracy. Despite these differences, however, the willingness of large numbers of people—particularly students, who represented the future of these developing nations—to engage in civil resistance in the face of brutal repression forced enlightened sectors of the military to recognize that it was no longer worth ruling by force.

5) Anti-Democratic Coups Following Civil Resistance-Initiated, Allegedly Pro-Democracy Coups

This section explores two cases, Sudan and Egypt, Scenario 5 (see page 16), where the military, facing a major civil insurrection, temporarily seizes power to oust a dictator and hands nominal power over to democratic forces—only to later take advantage of political divisions to seize power again and install a military dictatorship.

Sudan, April 1985 and June 1989

Sudan has a much-deserved reputation for the massive violence that has taken the lives of millions of people since the country gained its independence from Great Britain and Egypt in 1956. Yet this predominately Arab country experienced two of the world's earliest and most impressive successful nonviolent civil insurrections against dictatorship.

The first major Sudanese pro-democracy uprising took place against the regime of Field Marshal Ibrahim Abboud in October of 1964. When authorities tried to suppress the growing public debate regarding the legitimacy of the military government, which had ruled the country since 1958, large protests by a coalition of students, professionals, workers, leftists, nationalists and Islamists broke out. Within a week, a general strike had shut down the country.

On October 28, scores of nonviolent protesters in Khartoum were gunned down by government forces. Politicians and activists, through family and other personal ties, took advantage of a deepening split within the military to convince them to depose Abboud and return the country to civilian governance—which ultimately happened on October 30. A series of unstable civilian coalitions governed the country for the next five years, until the democratic government was deposed by a bloodless military coup in May 1969, led by Colonel Jafaar Nimeiry.

During the 16 years that followed, Nimeiry shifted his ideology from left-wing nationalist to pro-Western anti-communist, and then to Islamist, but never altered his increasingly unpopular and autocratic style of leadership. He established an internal security and intelligence force numbering 45,000 personnel under his direct control. He then gave them access to arms caches throughout the country and control over their own television, radio, and communications network, suppressing much of the opposition. Discontent grew in the early 1980s and, despite the growing repression, judges and lawyers successfully led strikes in 1983, and physicians the following year. Most observers, however, believed that Nimeiry was still firmly in control.

The Resistance

That changed, however, on March 26, 1985, when a series of massive and largely nonviolent demonstrations broke out in the capital of Khartoum and the neighboring city of Omdurman. Trade unions and professional organizations called a general strike, which ultimately paralyzed the country. At the same time the pro-democracy movement was gaining increasing support from a growing cross-section of the population, including the business community (see Table 9 on page 64).

Despite thousands of arrests and scores of shootings, the largely peaceful protests continued, with even the country's judiciary joining the civil rebellion. Protesters shut down pro-government radio stations and occupied airport runways to prevent Nimeiry, who was then on a state visit to Washington, from returning home. Pro-democracy activists stormed the notorious Kober prison and freed 400 political prisoners.

An anonymous group of "free officers" declared their solidarity with the pro-democracy movement, and secret negotiations between opposition leaders and high-ranking officers began. On April 3, the largest demonstration in the country's history took place as over one million people took to the streets of the capital. The military, faced with such a large civilian mobilization, refused to suppress the protests. On April 4, General Rahman Swar al-Dahab met with the opposition leadership, who succeeded in convincing him not to declare a state of emergency or use force to suppress the civil insurrection. The demonstrations were able to continue without interference. Meanwhile, opposition leaders from the trade unions, political parties, and professional associations gathered to draft a National Charter and elect a leadership.

The Coup and its Aftermath

On April 6, General al-Dahrab and other generals seized power in a military coup, formally overthrowing the dictator. Nimeiry, who had finally made his way into the country that day, fled into exile in Egypt. General al-Dahrab immediately dismantled his security force, confiscating their weapons and removing around 400 officers closest to the deposed dictator from their positions.

Not wanting military rule even without Nimeiry, however, pro-democracy activists continued their protests, forcing the new junta to establish a Transitional Military Council (TMC). The TMC was headed by General al-Dahab but consisted of a civilian cabinet of technocrats unaffiliated with major political parties and with the support of a broad coalition of opposition groups, professionals, and trade unionists. It was determined they would rule jointly for a year before free elections to determine a new government.

As with the earlier Sudanese experiment in democracy, however, the shaky civilian governments that followed were unable to unify the country. With divisions between conservative Islamists and left-leaning secular nationalists in the government growing, the military began to reassert its influence. The hardline Islamists, unable to win a majority through free elections, then allied themselves with the military. On June 30, 1989, Colonel Omar al-Bashir led a military coup, establishing the Revolutionary Command Council (RCC), suspending political parties and imposing an Islamic legal code on the nation. This was followed by a series of purges and executions of senior military officers, making the ban on political parties permanent, as well as forbidding independent organizations and newspapers. Leading journalists and political figures were imprisoned. By 1993, al-Bashir had consolidated power by naming himself president, disbanding the RCC, and assuming its executive and legislative powers.

Al-Bashir's military/Islamist regime has been more thorough than previous autocrats in terms of the systematic destruction of key civil society institutions, particularly trade unions, which played a major role in the 1964 and 1985 uprisings. Still, pro-democracy groups like Girifna (Arabic for "We are fed up") have continued to organize until the present day. In addition to armed regional rebellions in the west, south, and northeast in recent decades, there have also been periodic nonviolent struggles for greater democracy and accountability.

TABLE 9: SUDAN, 1985 AND 1989	
Main CR actors	Civil society organizations; trade unionists
Main coup proponents	Dictatorship
CR strategies & tactics	Protests; rallies; popular contestation of public space; strikes
Level of planning / strategic thought	Fairly high during initial uprising
Duration of the coup	12 months initially; then permanently
Duration of the CR	12 days
Level of nonviolent discipline	Generally high, though some rioting
Size of the movement/ diversity of anti-coup movement	Over one million, primarily in capital and nearby cities
Domestic allies and loyalty shifts	Professionals; Islamists; some segments of military
International allies/ community	Neutral
Type/rank of coup leaders	Generals
How military took over/ planned to take over	Forced president's resignation
Level of repression	Serious prior to coup; minimal in interim; severe following second coup
Mechanism of change	Deposed dictator
Short-term results and long-term impact of CR	Some liberalization, free elections initially; serious authoritarianism following second coup
What happened to the movement	Remained active following initial coup; largely crushed following second

Egypt, February 2011 and July 2013

At the turn of the new century, crushing poverty, increasing human rights abuses, rampant inflation, institutionalized corruption, a deteriorating educational system, and high unemployment spawned massive protests throughout Egypt. Between 1998 and 2010, more than two million Egyptians participated in over 3300 strikes, demonstrations, and factory occupations (Franklin, 2010). Many thousands poured into the streets of Cairo, Alexandria, and other major cities despite brutal police attacks on demonstrators, widespread torture of detainees, and other repressive measures. A 2007 sit-in involving 3000 municipal workers at the finance ministry ultimately won higher salaries and the right to form an independent union. In the spring of 2010, thousands of workers staged rotating sit-ins in front of the parliament building despite police efforts to disperse them by force. As protests grew, the government announced a freeze on further privatization and gave in on other economic demands.

This period witnessed a dramatic growth in Egyptian civil society, with an increasing number of labor strikes and small, but ever-larger, demonstrations led by such youthful, secular pro-democracy groups as Kefaya (meaning "Enough!") and the April 6 Movement (named after a nationwide strike and protest on that date in 2008). Towards the end of 2010, dissatisfaction with Mubarak was driven by increasing government repression, the police murder of a popular blogger for exposing government corruption, worsening economic conditions, blatantly rigged parliamentary elections, and the implication of security forces in a church bombing that appeared to have been designed to stoke sectarian tensions. Some activists believed that popular sentiments against the regime were deep and widespread enough that change was indeed possible. The successful uprising in Tunisia, leading to the downfall of the Ben Ali regime on January 14, 2011, led some Egyptians believe a similar uprising might be successful in their country as well.

The Resistance

A demonstration was scheduled for January 25, 2011, a national holiday honoring the country's (notoriously brutal and corrupt) police. Hundreds of feeder marches surged through the back alleys of Cairo, growing block by block. By the time they fed into Tahrir Square, they numbered in the tens of thousands, with hundreds of thousands joining them in subsequent days. Similar scenes unfolded throughout the country, as millions took to the streets in most of Egypt's major cities (see Table 10 on page 69). Police responded brutally, but protesters held Cairo's Tahrir Square and other key points in the country.

On January 17, the regime shut down virtually all Internet and mobile phone service, but the crowds continued to swell. While overwhelmingly peaceful, there was some rioting, looting and vandalism. On January 28, the headquarters of the ruling National Democratic Party were burned. A full-scale revolt was in progress. The police were overwhelmed and withdrew as the army was called in to try to maintain order. At first, the regime tried to appease the protesters with minor reforms. Mubarak appointed a vice president and reshuffled his cabinet. Three days later, he announced he would not seek re-election and that his son would not succeed him. Mubarak also announced that he would reform the constitution.

By this point, however, it appeared that nothing short of the downfall of the regime would satisfy protesters as the crowds swelled into the millions in cities and towns throughout the country—as many as 12 million Egyptians were on the streets demanding Mubarak's resignation. In Cairo, Alexandria, and elsewhere, the Mubarak regime unleashed its thugs to attack demonstrators, journalists and others. Government snipers gunned down hundreds of largely peaceful protesters. With the police in disarray after a mass release of criminals from prison, it appeared the government was deliberately sowing enough chaos that Egyptians would demand a strong government crackdown. By this time, however, the death toll was approaching one thousand, and international criticism was rising — including from the United States, the Mubarak regime's most important foreign backer. Despite initial hesitation, the Obama administration began quietly pushing for the dictator to step down.

The Coup and its Aftermath

Fearing that the growing uprising might not only eventually oust Mubarak but challenge the military's leading role in the country, Egyptian generals successfully forced Mubarak to resign on February 11 and formed an interim military government, the Supreme Council of the Armed Forces (SCAF). Over the next six months, smaller protests continued in Tahrir Square and elsewhere demanding more substantive political change until an army crackdown in August of 2011. A new round of pro-democracy protests in November was brutally suppressed.

Despite this, increasing press freedoms and civil liberties, along with upcoming competitive parliamentary and presidential elections, gave many Egyptians hope that a genuine democracy would eventually emerge. While the first round of presidential elections in 2012 resulted in a slight majority for more democratic and secular candidates, the top two candidates who made the runoff represented the military and the Muslim Brotherhood (Ikhwan). In the view of leaders of the pro-democracy uprising, this was the worst possible electoral outcome. Mohamed Morsi, the Ikhwan candidate, won the presidency with a narrow victory in the second round of voting.

The religious conservative Morsi failed to open his cabinet to non-Islamists and proved to be a not particularly competent or popular president. A November 2012 presidential decree that gave him extraordinary powers was seen as an autocratic power grab (Beaumont, 2013), even though his defenders argued it was temporary and designed to assert a degree of civilian primacy over the military and the corrupt judiciary. Quietly encouraged by the military, Egyptians poured into the streets once again, demanding new elections. When Morsi refused, they began calling for his ouster.

By July of 2013, popular anger at Morsi led Egypt's military to remove him in a coup. He had been president for only a year. The military grossly exaggerated the size of the protests, claiming that at 33 million, it was even higher than the protests against Mubarak. However, at the 20 major protests sites across Egypt between June 30 and July 3, a generous estimate using standard crowd-sizing methodology put the numbers as between two and three million (la Septième Wilaya, 2013). The most reliable polling data showed that, despite growing dissatisfaction, Morsi had slightly more than 50 percent support before the coup (Pew Research Center, 2013) and, even after the media barrage against him after the coup, he maintained a support rating of more than 40 percent (Zogby Research Services, 2013).

A brutal crackdown followed. More than 1000 supporters of the Muslim Brotherhood were massacred while engaging in a mostly peaceful sit-in the following month. Together with the Brotherhood and other Islamists, pro-democracy forces were suppressed as well. Many of the left-leaning secular leaders of the 2011 civil insurrection against Mubarak found themselves in prison. Presidential elections in May of 2014, widely criticized as neither free nor fair, resulted in the election of General Abdel Fattah el-Sisi, the commander who led the coup. El-Sisi has effectively prohibited protests and banned the leading pro-democracy groups, which had led the movement against Mubarak.

Since the coup, the military-led regime has killed more than 2000 demonstrators and arrested tens of thousands (Dunne and Williamson, 2014). They have severely restricted political rights and shut down opposition media (Youssef, 2013). The "elections" under their rule have been total shams, as they have banned or otherwise eliminated their only serious political competitors (Kirkpatrick, 2014). While the Ikhwan-backed 2012 Constitution, albeit imperfect, did provide a basis for a democratic system, the replacement constitution pushed through by the junta in 2014 codified the role of the Egyptian military as the nation's most powerful political player.

The 2011 coup was a defensive reaction to the massive popular wave of protests that had made the country ungovernable and threatened the military's traditional dominance. Mubarak would have almost certainly been forced out of power even if the military had not acted. By contrast, while popular opposition to Morsi was indeed strong and widespread, the military played an active role in encouraging the protests. It seized control despite the democratically elected Ikhwan government's still sizable popular base of support, the smaller numbers of demonstrators, and the possibility of being able to remain in power despite the protests. The military's second seizure of power, then, was more of a classic coup, as became evident when its leaders began suppressing not just their Islamist opponents, but secular pro-democracy groups as well in their consolidation of authoritarian rule.

Many Egyptians have embraced the new authoritarianism and support the Sisi regime. This is largely a result of two factors: first, opposition against the Muslim Brotherhood and the more extreme Islamists, and second, concern about the negative economic impact of years of protests and political instability. However, dissent is growing, especially among the younger generation opposed to both Islamic and military autocracy. They hunger for greater freedoms and social justice, and are cognizant of the power of large-scale strategic nonviolent action in bringing down dictatorship.

TABLE 10: EGYPT, 2011 AND 2013

Main CR actors	Secular civil society groups
Main coup proponents	Dictatorship
CR strategies & tactics	Protests; rallies; popular contestation of public space; strikes
Level of planning / strategic thought	Fairly high during initial uprising
Duration of the coup	14 months initially; then permanently
Duration of the CR	18 days
Level of nonviolent discipline	Moderate, some rioting
Size of the movement/ diversity of anti-coup movement	Millions; throughout urban areas of the country
Domestic allies and loyalty shifts	Professionals; trade unions; Islamists; some segments of military
International allies/ community	Mixed
Type/rank of coup leaders	Generals
How military took over/ planned to take over	Forced president's resignation
Level of repression	Serious prior to coup; moderate in interim; severe following second coup
Mechanism of change	Deposed and jailed dictator
Short-term results and long-term impact of CR	Some liberalization; free elections initially; seriously authoritarianism following second coup
What happened to the movement	Remained active following initial coup; largely crushed following second

Sudan and Egypt: Comparison and Conclusion

Though neighboring, predominantly Muslim and Arab states, there are distinct differences between the larger, more developed, and more homogenous Egypt and its impoverished multi-ethnic neighbor to the south. There are also differences in how the two countries failed to consolidate their democratic gains from the initial nonviolent uprisings. The Sudanese army's decision to remove Nimeiri was motivated by their recognition of the degree of alienation in the general population, which had led to large-scale civil resistance. They did not initially plan to turn over control to civilians, however, until continuing protests forced them to do so.

During the subsequent four years, they witnessed how factious civilian governments had difficulty governing. This was exacerbated by the failure of the United States and other countries to support the more independent-minded democratic coalition that was struggling with serious economic problems inherited from the old regime. Support from conservative civilian Islamist elements allowed hardline Islamist officers to gain broad enough support to seize power.

> *The Sudanese army did not initially plan to turn over control to civilians until continuing protests forced them to do so.*

Despite having served as a general and head of the Egyptian air force, Mubarak had been losing support in the military during his final years, particularly since he initiated efforts to promote his non-military son as his successor. As a result, the military did not hesitate to force his resignation in the face of massive protests and the withdrawal of U.S. support. The pro-democracy elements supporting the demonstrations were mostly willing to allow the military to take control following Mubarak's overthrow. Two main factors combined to account for this: First, broad naïveté about the military's intentions, and second, great respect for the Egyptian military dating back to Nasser and the Free Officers movement of the 1952 revolution. Concern over the political power of both the conservative Muslim Brotherhood as well as extremist Salafist elements—which were better organized and funded than the democratic secular elements—led many to believe that allying with the secular military was the only way to prevent the imposition of an Islamist-ruled Egypt. By the time the military had consolidated its power and began cracking down on the secular democrats, it was too late.

In both Sudan and Egypt, the militaries were able to consolidate power due to the weakness and divisions among civilian political leadership. Another factor was that a significant minority in both countries—tiring of economic and other problems resulting from years of political turmoil—preferred a strong autocratic government to a weak democratic government. The failure of the United States and other allied governments to support democratic forces more consistently also strengthened the military's hand in reconsolidating power.

The main problem in Sudan was the divisions among the opposition, particularly between secularists and Islamists, exacerbated by the country's ethnic divisions. In the case of Egypt, it was the unpopularity of the Muslim Brotherhood-controlled government and pro-democracy elements' naïve trust of the military that allowed the re-imposition of authoritarian rule. In both cases, despite the impressive utilization of civil resistance against great odds, it was the political failures subsequent to the largely nonviolent insurrections that doomed the brief democratic openings.

6) Unsuccessful Civil Resistance to Coups

Honduras, 2009

This section explores two cases, Honduras and The Maldives, Scenario 6 (see page 16), where civil resistance against coups was unsuccessful. Honduras emerged from decades of military dictatorship in the 1980s. Having largely been spared the brutal civil wars that had engulfed its neighbors, Honduras was able to have regular competitive elections, a relatively free press, and a burgeoning civil society movement, even though its governments tended to be fairly conservative in policies and plutocratic in leadership.

Despite being a wealthy logger and rancher from the centrist Liberal Party, Manuel Zelaya, elected in 2005, had moved his government to the left during his four years in office. During his tenure, he raised the minimum wage; provided free school lunches and milk for young children, pensions for the elderly; additional scholarships for students; built new schools; and subsidized public transportation, among other social welfare projects. While none of these were particularly radical moves, it was nevertheless disturbing to the country's wealthy economic and military elites.

More frightening was that Zelaya had sought to organize an assembly to replace the 1982 constitution written during the waning days of the U.S.-backed military dictator Policarpo Paz García. A non-binding referendum on whether such a constitutional assembly should take place was scheduled for June 28, 2009, but was cancelled when the military seized power, forcibly exiled Zelaya, and named Congressional Speaker Roberto Micheletti as president.

The Resistance

Immediately, thousands of protesters took to the streets in the capital of Tegucigalpa and other cities as the military imposed a curfew, along with restrictions on the media and public protests. Protests, along with strikes, spread across the country (see Table 11 on page 75). Internationally, the UN General Assembly and the Organization of American States condemned the coup, and foreign governments began recalling their ambassadors. On July 3, 2009, an estimated 100,000 people protested in Tegucigalpa. Protests continued the following day in the capital, as well as San Pedro Sula, Talanga, La Ceiba, El Progreso, Choluteca, and other cities.

Following the coup, thousands of Hondurans from diverse sectors of society gathered daily in the streets of Tegucigalpa and elsewhere, demanding the restoration of their democratically elected government—in most cases met by tear gas and truncheons. Over a dozen pro-democracy activists were murdered in the initial weeks, but rather than letting these assassinations frighten people into submission, the opposition turned the martyrs' funerals into political rallies. Their persistence raised questions both domestically and internationally regarding the regime's claims of legitimacy.

> *Feisty and determined acts of resistance forced the provisional government into clumsy efforts at repression—exposing the pretense of the junta's supposed good intentions.*

The Honduran opposition movement consisted of a hodgepodge of trade unionists, *campesinos* from the countryside, Afro-Hondurans, teachers, feminists, students, and others. In addition to insisting on the right of their elected president to return to office, they were determined to build a more just society. Prior to the coup, there had never been a national mobilization in Honduras lasting for more than a week, much less four months.

The forcibly exiled Zelaya announced he would attempt to return to Honduras to reclaim his presidency, calling on his supporters to remain peaceful, saying, "Do not bring weapons. Practice what I have always preached, which is nonviolence. Let them be the ones who use violence, weapons and repression" (Weissert, 2009). Tens of thousands of people went out to the airport to greet Zelaya as he attempted to return from exile. However, the military blocked the runways preventing the plane from landing and brutally attacked demonstrators, killing two. Over 600 people were arrested.

The sustained nonviolent resistance movement initially prevented the provisional government formed after the June 28 coup from fully consolidating power. Demonstrations continued throughout the country along with blockades of major highways. While the movement was lacking in well-organized, strategic focus, feisty and determined acts of resistance forced the provisional government into clumsy efforts at repression—exposing the pretense of the junta's supposed good intentions. By simply staying alive, the resistance was able to prevent a sense of normalcy in the country. A flurry of diplomatic activity brought forward a number of compromise proposals.

On September 21, Zelaya snuck back into the country and successfully sought refuge in the Brazilian embassy, revitalizing the pro-democracy movement. The Micheletti regime initially panicked—suspending basic civil liberties, shutting down opposition radio and television stations, and declaring a 24-hour curfew. This disruption caused the business community's support for the de facto government to wane; the U.S. State Department under Obama, which had been somewhat timid in pressing the junta up to that point, began to push harder for a deal. With the exception of occasional small-

Demonstrators at an undisclosed location in Honduras, June 29, 2009. Credit: Flickr user Yamil Gonzales (CC BY-SA 2.0).

scale rioting, the movement largely maintained its nonviolent discipline. Despite serious provocations by police and soldiers loyal to the provisional government, the movement recognized that armed resistance would have been utterly futile and counter-productive.

On October 30, an agreement was reached in which Zelaya would be allowed to temporarily return to power pending elections in which he was not a candidate, but the junta reneged on its agreement and instead went ahead with a national election on November 30. While most Latin American countries opposed moving ahead with an election while restrictions on civil liberties remained in place, Colombia and other conservative governments, along with the United States, appeared willing to recognize it.

The elections, held under military rule and marred by violence and media censorship (Weisbrot, 2009), were hardly free or fair (Vickers, 2009). The Union of South American Nations (UNASUR) declared they would not recognize elections held under the de facto government. The Organization of American States drafted a resolution that would have refused to recognize Honduran elections carried out under the dictatorship, but the United States blocked its adoption. A conservative pro-coup candidate won with a less than 50% turnout.

The Aftermath

In the subsequent years, repression has continued, thousands of indigenous activists, peasant leaders, trade unionists, journalists, environmentalists, judges, opposition political candidates, human rights activists, and others have been assassinated. Political repression has continued and the skyrocketing murder rate—now the second highest in the world (UNDOC, 2015)—has resulted in tens of thousands of refugees fleeing the country for safety.

Despite this, civil society movements continue to push for human rights and environmental protection. Elections in 2013 resulted in the re-election of the conservative National Party which had held power since 2009 against centrist and liberal opposition candidates. However, there were serious concerns about the fairness of the vote given the endemic violence against opposition party activists, the increasing role of the military in policing functions, and the ruling party's monopolistic control on military, judiciary and electoral authority (Carasick, 2013). Attempts by right-wing incumbent president Juan Orlando Hernandez, a prominent supporter of the 2009 coup, to steal the 2017 election were met with large-scale civil resistance.

TABLE 11: HONDURAS, 2009	
Main CR actors	Supporters of deposed president
Main coup proponents	Military; opposition conservative party
CR strategies & tactics	Protests; blockades; noncooperation
Level of planning / strategic thought	Weak
Duration of the coup	Ongoing
Duration of the CR	5 months
Level of nonviolent discipline	High
Size of the movement/ diversity of anti-coup movement	Hundreds of thousands; throughout urban areas of the country
Domestic allies and loyalty shifts	Trade unionists; members of deposed party; indigenous groups; leftists
International allies/ community	Mixed; most nations opposed; U.S. supportive
Type/rank of coup leaders	Supreme Court; Congressional leaders
How military took over/ planned to take over	Arrested and exiled president
Level of repression	Moderate to severe
Mechanism of change	Allies of putschists still in power
Short-term results and long-term impact of CR	Flawed elections; semi-autocratic system
What happened to the movement	Civil society groups remain active despite ongoing targeted killings

The Maldives, 2012

Years of widespread nonviolent resistance against the 30-year reign of the corrupt and autocratic president Maldivian president Maumoon Abdul Gayoom eventually forced the dictator to allow free elections in October of 2008, which he lost.

When the democratic opposition leader and former political prisoner Mohamed Nasheed assumed the presidency, he was faced with the difficult task of repairing the country's damaged social fabric from decades of misrule. While luxury resorts had mushroomed on many of the Maldives' remote islands, most of the population suffered in poverty. Indeed, Gayoom's legacy has been one of shattered communities, destitution, crime, and widespread drug abuse. Despite their best efforts, Nasheed and his democratic allies were hampered by a court system still dominated by corrupt judges whom the former dictator had handpicked, as well as violent protests by Islamists angered at the democratic government's moderate social policies. Meanwhile, despite struggles at home, Nasheed took global leadership in pushing for concrete international action on climate change, through which rising sea levels threaten his nation's very existence.

Nasheed's increasingly bold and popular efforts against the vestiges of the Gayoom dictatorship, however, threatened powerful interests. On February 7, 2012, police and other security forces with links to the old regime, in alliance with Vice President Mohammed Waheed, forced President Nasheed to sign a letter of resignation. Subsequent evidence leaves little doubt that Nasheed was accurate in describing it as a coup d'état. Vice President Waheed, who was apparently part of the plot, assumed the presidency and promptly dismissed Nasheed's ministers, replacing them with conservative Islamists opposed to Nasheed's liberal reforms as well as nine key figures from the former dictatorship, including Gayoom's son and daughter (Kurukulasuriya, 2012).

The United States immediately recognized the new government and refused to acknowledge the coup by referring to the ouster of the democratically elected president as simply a "transition of power." Similarly, U.S. State Department spokesman Victoria Nuland commended as "thorough and conclusive" a highly problematic Commission of Inquiry which claimed Nasheed's resignation was not under duress—despite its failure to consider important evidence to the contrary or allow for key witnesses (Naseem, 2012).

The Resistance

Upon Nasheed's forced removal, protests immediately broke out throughout the archipelago, with thousands going out daily for protests in support of the constitutional government. In response, more than 2000 peaceful protesters were arrested—an extremely high number for a country with a population of barely 350,000—many suffering severe beatings at the hands of security forces (see Table 12 on page 79). Amnesty International has described the situation in the Maldives as a "human rights crisis", documenting security force brutality and arbitrary arrests (Amnesty International, 2016a). Major leaders of Nasheed's party have been arrested on politically motivated charges and the media has been censored.

Despite increased repression under the provisional government, pro-democracy activists continued their nonviolent struggle, forcing the junta to allow for new elections in September 2013. Despite harassment and periodic detention, Nasheed was able to organize a campaign based on democratic rights, tax reforms, and sustainable development.

As a result of apparent ballot stuffing and other fraudulent procedures documented by independent journalists and other observers, Nasheed fell just short of a majority and the runoff was cancelled. A second election, under dubious circumstances, led to his defeat. In February of 2015, just days before he was to lead a mass demonstration against the regime, Nasheed was arrested on trumped-up charges of "terrorism" and sentenced to 13 years in prison. Another series of protests scheduled for November of that year were suppressed with the government declaring a state of emergency and banning any opposition political gatherings.

The Aftermath

The repression has largely stifled the opposition, as opponents have been jailed on politically motivated charges, travel restrictions have been imposed, and unprecedented restrictions have been placed on the media. An international tourist boycott has received some support and, despite initial backing for the military-backed government, foreign governments have begun expressing concern over ongoing autocratic rule. Maldives withdrew from the British Commonwealth of Nations in response to growing criticism of the deteriorating human rights situation from its members (Amnesty International, 2016b). Despite disastrous economic policies and aid from the ultra-conservative Saudi regime have kept the government solvent and the economy afloat.

The geography of the country—consisting of an archipelago over hundreds of small islands—makes it relatively easy for the regime to restrict movement. The capital of Malé is on an island of less than six square kilometers, making it easy to locate dissidents. Drug addiction is a major problem, with some estimates showing that as many as 40% of those under 30 use heroin, greatly limiting the ability to organize a sector of the population that has traditionally played a disproportionate role in pro-democracy struggles (Radio Netherlands Worldwide). Still, resistance is continuing, and with the precedent of having brought down the Gayoum regime in 2008, pro-democracy activists still hope for eventual victory.

TABLE 12: THE MALDIVES, 2012

Main CR actors	Supporters of deposed president
Main coup proponents	Military; opposition conservative party
CR strategies & tactics	Protests; noncooperation
Level of planning / strategic thought	Weak
Duration of the coup	Ongoing
Duration of the CR	Sporadic for 2+ years
Level of nonviolent discipline	High
Size of the movement/ diversity of anti-coup movement	Thousands, primarily in capital
Domestic allies and loyalty shifts	Civil society groups; members of deposed party
International allies/ community	Largely neutral
Type/rank of coup leaders	Vice president
How military took over/ planned to take over	Forced president's resignation
Level of repression	Moderate to severe
Mechanism of change	Putschists still in power
Short-term results and long-term impact of CR	Flawed elections; semi-autocratic system
What happened to the movement	Civil society groups weakened but remain active despite ongoing repression

Honduras and the Maldives: Comparison and Conclusion

In the cases of the Maldives and Honduras, relatively strong civil society movements were nevertheless unable to reverse the coups. Mobilization in the Maldives was hampered in part due to the geographical limitations of being an archipelago of tiny islands. As for Honduras, paramilitary groups allied with the regime suppressed the mobilization with assassinations and death threats.

One problem that hurt both pro-democracy struggles was that the democratically elected presidents' ouster did not fit the model of a classic military takeover, given that the most prominent putschists were civilians who were able to use a legal cover for their seizure of power. Though a strong case can be made for the illegitimacy of the two coups, both domestic and foreign opponents of the ousted civilian government were able to use the perceived legal ambiguity to their advantage.

Like other coup resisters examined in this monograph, the pro-democracy forces in these two countries faced the challenge of having to mobilize quickly under repressive circumstances. They were also forced to deal with a politically divided citizenry and inadequate international support. All these factors made it impossible for the coup resisters in Honduras and the Maldives to achieve their victory. At the same time, despite these enormous odds, resisters did significantly increase the costs for the coup instigators and made it possible for citizens and the international community to question regime legitimacy.

Part 2
Generalized Findings from the Analyzed Cases

The 12 studied cases outlined and compared in Table 13 on the following pages underscore Sharp's and Jenkins's assertions that there is an important distinction between seizing the physical control of government facilities and exercising effective political control over the state. Even in the Argentine and Russian cases where putschists were able to seize key facilities, it soon became apparent they were still unable to control the rest of the country due to lack of popular support.

All of the movements challenging coups in this monograph partially implemented the specific strategies and tactics that Sharp and Jenkins describe to varying degrees. However, none did so comprehensively or thoroughly. In each case, only a small minority of the population was actively involved in the resistance. Yet even a limited degree of defiance and noncooperation was enough in the successful cases to prevent the putschists from consolidating power.

These successful cases appear to reconfirm much of the literature on civil resistance compiled from case studies of strategic nonviolent action against long-running dictatorships. In addition to Sharp's (1973) findings on the centrality of noncooperation, these studies validate more recent research as well, including the phenomenon of "backfire," where state repression strengthens rather than weakens the pro-democracy movement (Martin, 2007); the importance of movement resilience in the face of repression and threats thereof, and the resulting leverage (Schock, 2005); the size of protests as a determining factor (Chenoweth and Stephan, 2011); the coherence (or defections) of the military in the face of challenges; and the role played by religious institutions (Nepstad, 2011).

While a number of variables contributed to the success or failure of these struggles, the effective use of civil resistance in challenging the attempted seizure of power by undemocratic elements appears to be by far the most critical factor in coup collapse.

Table 13: Twelve Case Studies Compared

	MAIN CR ACTORS	MAIN ACTORS CR OPPOSED
SOVIET UNION, 1991	Reformist political leaders; liberal civil society elements; citizens and officials of Baltic republics	Conservative Communist Party leaders
THAILAND, 1992	Civilian political leaders; professionals; Buddhists; pro-democracy activists	Military junta
FRANCE, 1961	Elected civilian leadership; civil society; trade unionists; lower ranks of military	Military putschists; French colonists in Algeria
ARGENTINA, 1987	Elected civilian leadership; civil society; trade unionists	Military putschists
BOLIVIA, 1978	Pro-democracy activists; trade unionists; urban working class; civilian politicians	Military junta
BURKINA FASO, 2015	Pro-democracy activists; civilian politicians; some military	Military junta; leaders of former ruling party
VENEZUELA, 1958	Civil society organizations	Military dictatorship
MALI, 1991	Major opposition party; students	Military dictatorship
SUDAN, 1985 and 1989	Civil society organizations; trade unionists	Dictatorship
EGYPT, 2011 and 2013	Secular civil society groups	Dictatorship
HONDURAS, 2009	Supporters of deposed president	Military; opposition conservative party
THE MALDIVES, 2012	Supporters of deposed president	Military; opposition conservative party

Table 13: Twelve Case Studies Compared

	CR STRATEGIES AND TACTICS	LEVEL OF PLANNING / STRATEGIC THOUGHT
SOVIET UNION, 1991	Noncooperation; protests; contestation of public space	Russia: Moderate (largely spontaneous, leadership by reformist politicians); Baltics: High
THAILAND, 1992	Petitioning; protests; fasting; noncooperation	High
FRANCE, 1961	Noncooperation; strikes	Moderate
ARGENTINA, 1987	Noncooperation; blockades; street protests; strikes	Moderate
BOLIVIA, 1978	Noncooperation; protests; strikes; contestation of public space	High (re-mobilization of forces from recent pro-democracy struggle)
BURKINA FASO, 2015	Protests; blockades; strikes; noncooperation	Moderate (re-mobilization of forces from recent pro-democracy struggle)
VENEZUELA, 1958	Protests; general strike; confronting security forces	Moderate (underground organizations; call for general strike)
MALI, 1991	Protests; rallies; general strike	Moderate (decentralized clandestine organizations; consciousness-raising)
SUDAN, 1985 and 1989	Protests; rallies; popular contestation of public space; strikes	High
EGYPT, 2011 and 2013	Protests; rallies; popular contestation of public space; strikes	High
HONDURAS, 2009	Protests; blockades; noncooperation	Moderate
THE MALDIVES, 2012	Protests; noncooperation	Moderate

Table 13: Twelve Case Studies Compared

	DURATION OF THE MILITARY UPRISING / GOVERNANCE	DURATION OF CR	LEVEL OF NONVIOLENT DISCIPLINE
SOVIET UNION, 1991	3 days	3 days	High
THAILAND, 1992	15 months	41 days	Moderate (some arson and rioting)
FRANCE, 1961	4 days	4 days	High
ARGENTINA, 1987	3 days	3 days	High
BOLIVIA, 1978	16 days	16 days	Moderate (some rioting)
BURKINA FASO, 2015	7 days	7 days	High (though loyal army units utilized to arrest putschists)
VENEZUELA, 1958	11 months	3 weeks	Moderate (rioting and clashes with government forces)
MALI, 1991	13 months	5 days	Moderate (some rioting)
SUDAN, 1985 and 1989	12 months initially; then permanently	12 days	High (some rioting)
EGYPT, 2011 and 2013	14 months initially; then permanently	18 days	Moderate (some arson; rioting; clashes)
HONDURAS, 2009	Ongoing	5 months	High
THE MALDIVES, 2012	Ongoing	Sporadic for 2+ years	High

Table 13: Twelve Case Studies Compared

	SIZE AND DIVERSITY OF THE MOVEMENT	DOMESTIC ALLIES AND LOYALTY SHIFTS
SOVIET UNION, 1991	Hundreds of thousands; primarily in major cities and Baltic republics	Liberal elements in Communist Party; Baltic governments; media
THAILAND, 1992	Hundreds of thousands; throughout urban areas of the country	Civil society groups
FRANCE, 1961	Millions	Broad cross-section of French society
ARGENTINA, 1987	Millions, primarily in capital	Broad cross-section of Argentine society
BOLIVIA, 1978	Close to 1 million, nearly one-fifth of the population; including indigenous and mestizo	Broad cross-section of Bolivian society
BURKINA FASO, 2015	Hundreds of thousands; throughout urban areas of the country	Civil society groups; trade unions; most politicians; some segments of military
VENEZUELA, 1958	Hundreds of thousands; throughout urban areas of the country	Opposition political parties; professionals; Church; unions; some segments of military
MALI, 1991	Hundreds of thousands; throughout urban areas of the country	Young professionals; trade unions; some segments of military
SUDAN, 1985 and 1989	Over 1 million; primarily in capital and nearby cities	Professionals; Islamists; some segments of military
EGYPT, 2011 and 2013	Millions; throughout urban areas of the country	Professionals; trade unions; Islamists; some segments of military
HONDURAS, 2009	Hundreds of thousands; throughout urban areas of the country	Trade unionists; members of deposed party; indigenous groups; leftists
THE MALDIVES, 2012	Thousands; primarily in capital	Civil society groups; members of deposed party

Table 13: Twelve Case Studies Compared

	INTERNATIONAL RESPONSE TO COUP	TYPE / RANK OF COUP LEADERS	HOW MILITARY TOOK OVER
SOVIET UNION, 1991	Near-universal opposition to coup	Marshall of Soviet armed forces and hardline Communist leaders	Seized government buildings
THAILAND, 1992	Largely neutral	Military leadership	Seized government buildings and state apparatus
FRANCE, 1961	Widespread opposition	Right-wing army generals	Seized military bases and government offices in Algeria
ARGENTINA, 1987	Widespread opposition	Right-wing army generals	Seized military bases
BOLIVIA, 1978	Largely neutral	Army general	Seized government buildings; attacking opposition strongholds
BURKINA FASO, 2015	Largely negative; opposition led by regional organization	General of presidential guard	Seized government buildings; held leading officials hostage
VENEZUELA, 1958	Neutral	General and commander of armed forces	Forced president's resignation
MALI, 1991	Neutral	Lieutenant colonel	Seized government buildings
SUDAN, 1985 and 1989	Neutral	Generals	Forced president's resignation
EGYPT, 2011 and 2013	Mixed	Generals	Forced president's resignation
HONDURAS, 2009	Mixed: most nations opposed; U.S. supportive	Supreme Court; Congressional leaders	Arrested and exhiled president
THE MALDIVES, 2012	Largely neutral	Vice president	Forced president's resignation

Table 13: Twelve Case Studies Compared

	LEVEL OF REPRESSION	MECHANISM OF CHANGE
SOVIET UNION, 1991	Moderate	Forced resignation due to lack of support
THAILAND, 1992	Moderate to high	Resignation of appointed leaders; withdrawal to barracks
FRANCE, 1961	Low	Arrest of leaders
ARGENTINA, 1987	Low	Arrest of leaders
BOLIVIA, 1978	Moderate to high	Forced resignation due to mass noncooperation
BURKINA FASO, 2015	Moderate to high	Withdrew to barracks; later arrested
VENEZUELA, 1958	High prior to coup; minimal thereafter	Refusal to suppress uprising; demanding president's departure
MALI, 1991	High prior to coup; minimal thereafter	Deposed and jailed dictator
SUDAN, 1985 and 1989	Moderate to high prior to coup; minimal in interim; high following second coup	Deposed dictator
EGYPT, 2011 and 2013	Moderate to high prior to coup; moderate in interim; severe following second coup	Deposed and jailed dictator
HONDURAS, 2009	Moderate to high	Allies of putschists still in power
THE MALDIVES, 2012	Moderate to high	Putschists still in power

Table 13: Twelve Case Studies Compared

	SHORT-TERM RESULTS AND LONG-TERM IMPACT	WHAT HAPPENED TO THE MOVEMENT
SOVIET UNION, 1991	Abolition of ruling part; breakup of federal republic; mixed levels of democracy, autocracy and semi-autocracy in successor republics	Leaders came to power
THAILAND, 1992	Democratic elections and institutions for the next 14 years followed by series of military coups, CR, and democratic elections; currently under military rule	Civil society groups remain active
FRANCE, 1961	Maintaining democracy and preventing potential civil war	Civil society groups remain active
ARGENTINA, 1987	Maintaining democracy	Civil society groups remain active
BOLIVIA, 1978	Restoration of democracy for 21 months, followed by a successful coup, which was eventually brought down 3 years later; subsequent democracy	Remained strong; challenged a more serious coup 2 years later
BURKINA FASO, 2015	Democratic elections and institutions still in place	Civil society groups remain active
VENEZUELA, 1958	Democratic elections and institutions developed	Civil society organizations remained, though political involvement decreased
MALI, 1991	Democratic elections and institutions remained strong until 2012; more mixed subsequently	Civil society groups remain active
SUDAN, 1985 and 1989	Some liberalization; free elections initially; serious authoritarianism following second coup	Remained active following initial coup; largely crushed following second
EGYPT, 2011 and 2013	Some liberalization; free elections initially; serious authoritarianism following second coup	Remained active following initial coup; largely crushed following second
HONDURAS, 2009	Flawed elections; semi-autocratic system	Civil society groups remain active despite ongoing targeted killings
THE MALDIVES, 2012	Flawed elections; semi-autocratic system	Civil society groups weakened but remain active despite ongoing repression

Part 2: Generalized Findings from the Analyzed Cases

The coups that were defeated were those in which citizens successfully denied legitimacy to the putschists and resisted their attempted rule with noncooperation and defiance. Furthermore, the continued, active civil society engagement, including the use of civil resistance, appears to have been a critical variable in consolidating democratic gains after the coup disintegration. The refusal of local governments, independent social institutions, and the general population to cooperate with illegitimate authority can make it impossible for the putschists to effectively consolidate power and establish effective control over the country.

Despite enormous poverty and ethnic divisions afflicting their countries, the resistance movements in Bolivia and Burkina Faso were able to take advantage of existing networks, previous experience in civil resistance, and demonstrated popular will for a democratic future to successfully reverse coup attempts in a matter of days.

> *The coups that were defeated were those in which citizens successfully denied legitimacy to the putschists and resisted their attempted rule with noncooperation and defiance.*

The more developed societies in Russia and Thailand, despite no such recent uprisings, were nevertheless able to compensate by taking advantage of new communication technologies—cell phones in the case of Thailand and broadcast media in the case of Russia—to get the word out about the growing resistance. All four movements were able to successfully encourage noncooperation and resistance among government workers and the media and coax significant segments of the security forces to their side.

In the cases of Egypt and Sudan, in which the military initially helped oust a discredited dictatorship but later took control in a second coup, the military was able to take advantage of public desire for order and stability after a period of disruption, exploit divisions between progressive secular and conservative religious elements, and make alliances with key civilian sectors. In contrast, military leaders in Venezuela and Mali recognized that they were unable to sufficiently strengthen their support among the people or weaken that of pro-democracy elements, so they were forced to conclude that whatever restrictions on their power and privilege may result from democratic governance, they simply did not have the strength to easily retake power.

The successful cases of resistance and consolidation of democratic gains all involved large numbers of participants constituting a discernable proportion of the country's population and a broad cross-section of society. A partial exception was the

Soviet Union, which experienced proportionally smaller numbers than the other anti-coup movements, but were bolstered by the massive mobilizations in the crucial urban centers in Russia (mainly in Moscow and Leningrad) as well as in other Soviet republics such as the Baltic States. Such high participation forced even the local Communist leadership in these republics to declare independence in defiance of the putschists.

All successful cases of coup reversals included large public demonstrations and noncooperation. General strikes played an important role in Bolivia, Burkina Faso, France, Argentina, Mali, and in the initial uprisings in Sudan and Egypt. Blockades and popular contestation of public space, which crippled the economy and restricted normal transit (and, in some cases, movement of troops), played an important role in Bolivia, Burkina Faso, Argentina, Mali, Sudan, and Egypt. What all the uprisings had in common, however, was noncooperation. Public protests demonstrated public opposition and the "mood of the street", and blockades disrupted normal operations, but what ultimately left the putschists powerless was when they were faced with a sufficient degree of noncooperation.

Almost all successful uprisings ousted or ended the coups in a remarkably short period of three to 16 days. The exception was Thailand, where—initially believing claims that military rule was a temporary measure—pro-democracy forces mobilized only after a proposed constitutional change revealed the military's plan to stay in power. With the junta having been ensconced in power for more than a year, it then took more than 40 days of protests to force the regime to step down.

In each of the anti-democratic coups, the coup plotters included high-ranking military officers. With the exception of the Soviet Union, where the instigators were conservative Communist Party leaders (albeit with support of the Marshal of the Soviet armed forces), the coups were initiated by army generals or, in the case of Mali, the general commanding the presidential guard. Significantly, the coups where the putschists were able to resist civil resistance were those led primarily by conservative autocratic-minded civilians, in which they presented a constitutional façade for their takeover through the use of corrupt judges and legislative bodies, albeit with backing of senior military officers.

Overall, it appears that successful civil resistance campaigns against coups d'état indeed help create sustained democratic institutions and seem to significantly increase the likelihood for more peaceful and democratic order in the country within the first five or so years after a popular upheaval (see Table 14 on page 91). Using data from the Polity IV Individual Country Regime Trends to examine the level of democratic authority in governing institutions, countries in which popular movements reversed coups scored dramatic gains over the subsequent five years and countries in which popular movements prevented coups in progress maintained their already existing high levels.

Table 14: Democratic Gains Estimate

COUP & CIVIL RESISTANCE AFFECTED COUNTRY	DEMOCRATIC AUTHORITY SCORE PRIOR TO CIVIL RESISTANCE CAMPAIGN	DEMOCRATIC AUTHROITY SCORE FIVE YEARS LATER	NET CHANGE IN DEMOCRATIC AUTHORITY
RUSSIA (SOVIET UNION)	0 (1990)	3 (1995)	+ 3
THAILAND	- 1 (1992)	9 (1997)	+ 10
FRANCE	5 (1961)	5 (1966)	0
ARGENTINA	8 (1987)	7 (1992)	- 1
BOLIVIA	8 (1981)	- 7 (1986)	+ 15
BURKINA FASO	N/A	0 (2015)	N/A
VENEZUELA	- 3 (1958)	6 (1963)	+ 9
MALI	- 7 (1991)	7 (1996)	+ 14

Source: http://www.systemicpeace.org/polity/polity4x.htm

In eight countries, pro-democracy uprisings successfully prevented coups or prompted coups against incumbent dictatorships, which ultimately handed power over to civilian democrats. Six of the eight countries are to this day electoral democracies. Bolivia experienced another coup less than two years after it successfully reversed the Natusch Bush coup, but sustained civil resistance eventually restored democracy three years later. The 2012 coup in Mali, which took place after more than two decades of democratic rule, was eventually reversed, though ongoing armed conflict with Islamist extremists has weakened some democratic institutions. Thailand experienced democratic civilian governance for the first 15 years after the 1991 coup reversal. However, it is currently under military rule after several subsequent years of competing civil resistance campaigns between two main electoral blocs that politically polarized the country and led to the ousting by the military of two elected governments.

While Russia, the recognized successor state of the Soviet Union, is autocratic, eight of the 14 other former Soviet republics are electoral democracies, with Ukraine, Georgia, and Kyrgyzstan later experiencing pro-democracy civil insurrections against their own semi-autocratic rules. Not coincidentally, the Baltic republics of Lithuania, Latvia, and Estonia—which had the strongest civil resistance movements prior to the breakup of the Soviet Union—are the most viable democracies in the former Soviet space.

Part 3
Takeaways for Specific Practitioner Groups

Activists and Civil Society Groups

For pro-democracy activists and civil society groups, these cases help illustrate that active protests, even if simply through street demonstrations and other visible acts of resistance, can play an important role in signaling the general population's lack of recognition of the coup. This emboldens key elements of the government and security forces as well as international actors to oppose the takeover. More significant, however, is mobilizing large-scale non-recognition and noncooperation with the putschists' claim of governing authority. While physically occupying a government building or an important geographical point can have some symbolic advantages, what is important is defending the constitutional system, not a particular building. Indeed, the goal of pro-democracy resistance should be about defending society, not a particular physical location. And the defense of society under threat of a coup relies on widespread mobilization, building alliances, nonviolent discipline, and a refusal to recognize illegitimate authority.

Building Societal Capacity Against Coups

Given that (with the exception of the Soviet Baltic republics) none of these cases had the benefit of extensive pre-planning, it raises the question of how many successful coups in recent years could have been prevented or defeated quickly had the population been prepared to resist. Unfortunately, few people are even aware of these cases, much less what they can learn from them. Countries spend massive amounts of money to prepare for war against foreign enemies or suppression of domestic terrorists, but not to defend against coups—which historically are much greater tangible threats. Public awareness, combined with strengthening civic mobilization capacities would make it easier to reverse coups and could possibly even serve as a deterrent against coup attempts. If potential coup plotters knew the population was prepared to resist, they would be less inclined to try to usurp power.

Building societal capacity against coups could take various forms, for example mapping strengths and weaknesses of autonomous civil society and brainstorming what could be improved to enable quick civilian-led, independent mobilization. Schools could offer classes on civic activism and nonviolent actions, with additional after-school activities on civic engagement and strategic planning for effective campaigns. Specialized trainings could be organized for key civil society actors, such as workers in transit, communication, education, major industry, and other key sectors. The trainings could aim to develop a greater understanding of concepts in civil resistance, strategic communication, and coalition building; enable rapid deployment of civic and professional networks; and help mobilize material resources. A public awareness campaign could use popular movies, literature, entertainment and educational programs on television, radio or through social media to educate people on what to do should an attempted coup take place. Existing networks of civil society actors that are involved in various types of civic campaigns could prepare to be quickly utilized and repurposed to defend against a military takeover.

Security Forces and Government Civil Servants

For security services and governments workers, the key lesson is that, in order to defeat a coup, the putschists must be denied legitimacy and cooperation. Even if they are able to physically control government buildings, transportation centers, media centers and other key geographical locations, they still do not necessarily control the population or even government institutions, including security forces, if their legitimacy is not recognized. In order to function as the government, the putschists need the help of police, soldiers, prison guards, bureaucrats, technical specialists, generalists and advisors. To enforce their edicts, they need the cooperation of administrators, lawyers and judges. In order to communicate with the subjected population, they need the services of journalists, broadcasters and the technicians that run the media. Denial of such cooperation makes it impossible to rule.

Civil servants in key sectors of the government could be trained on how to refuse cooperation or engage in deliberate inefficiencies in case of military takeover. This could begin through general education that public servants must prioritize the good of the society rather than the interest of a small group of ruling elites. It could expand to providing information about examples and possibilities of collective and individual disobedience actions, both overt and subtle, in the event of a coup and how they might work in solidarity with the popular opposition.

External State Actors/International Community

Given the importance of international recognition to a government's legitimacy and its ability to engage in normal diplomatic and economic relations, the response of the international community to coup and coup attempts is of critical importance. In the case of Bolivia, the international community's reaction was muted and putschists would have likely received recognition had they been able to consolidate power. In Thailand in 1992, the military government was largely recognized after its initial seizure of power prior to the subsequent civil resistance campaign the following year. The international community's reaction was mixed to the second coups in Sudan and Egypt, while there was strong international opposition to the coup attempts in Burkina Faso, the Soviet Union, France, and Argentina. Though international opposition to the ongoing political repression in the Maldives has grown, the takeover and delayed presidential election was recognized as legitimate by important international actors. While initial international opposition to the Honduras coup was greater, there was sufficient support—particularly by the United States, long a powerful player in Central American affairs—for the dubious elections that followed to be recognized as legitimate.

International support for pro-democracy elements, particularly given the short window of opportunity that is usually open for civil society to prevent coup consolidation, is an important but not decisive factor in reversing a coup. Supporters of democratic movements abroad can play a role in encouraging their respective governments to back up democratic forces or at least refuse to recognize the putschists' governments. The more visible civil resistance to coup attempts is, the more difficult it is for foreign governments to legitimize putschists' rule. Indeed, advances in communication technologies and social media in recent decades have served to amplify civil resistance.

As a preventative measure, there are opportunities for democratic states, as part of their military-to-military collaboration with undemocratic counterparts and their armed forces, to help instill democratic values and the professional ethos of serving the nation, not the power of the day (Blair, 2013).

This Monograph as an Educational Instrument against Coups

Coup attempts are generally only made when the putschists believe they will face only minimal resistance, so the populations of countries potentially vulnerable to coups need to be prepared and organized enough to let any potential putschists know otherwise. As a result, the more awareness of successful coup reversals and the reasons for their success is known, the more likely democratic nations can defend themselves from such internal threats. Indeed, research indicates—and as game theory would predict—that soldiers' and officers' decisions to support or oppose a military coup is based less on ideology as it is on their sense of the likelihood that the coup will succeed or fail and how it would impact them personally (Singh, 2014). As a result, broadening our understanding of how a population can defeat a coup and how civil society can mobilize against a coup attempt improves the likelihood that major components of the military would refuse to support a coup attempt. By trying to understand the dynamics and importance of civil resistance to unlawful seizures of power by undemocratic forces, this monograph advances its own normative goal of educating and encouraging the readers to think how they, their communities and societies can better prepare themselves to be able to push nonviolently against the military, its parts or its civilian proxies when they usurp political power and curtail civil liberties.

Bibliography

Amnesty International, "Maldives: State of emergency an alarming development in continuing crackdown on human rights," November 4, 2015, https://www.amnesty.org/en/latest/news/2015/11/maldives-state-of-emergency-an-alarming-development-in-continuing-crackdown-on-human-rights/.

Amnesty International, "Maldives: Stop blaming others for rights record," October 13, 2016, https://www.amnesty.org/en/latest/news/2016/10/maldives-stop-blaming-others-for-rights-record/.

Bartkowski, Maciej (2015), *Nonviolent Civilian Defense to Counter Russian Hybrid Warfare* (published white paper). Washington, DC: Johns Hopkins University.

Beaumont, Peter, "Protests erupt across Egypt after presidential decree," *The Guardian*, November 23, 2012, https://www.theguardian.com/world/2012/nov/23/protests-egypt-presidential-decree.

Bertrand, Eloise, "Popular resistance to the Burkina Faso coup: who, where and what next?" *African Arguments*, September 21, 2015.

Blair, Dennis, "Military Engagement: Influencing Armed Forces Worldwide to Support Democratic Transitions". Washington, DC: Brookings Institution Press, 2013.

Bonkoungou, Mathieu and Bavier, Joe, "Burkina Faso presidential guard should be disbanded, panel says". *Reuters*, September 14, 2015, http://uk.reuters.com/article/uk-burkina-army-idUKKCN0RE2BN20150914.

Bonkoungou, Mathieu and Nadoun Coulibaly, "Burkina Faso army heads for capital to disarm coup leaders", *Reuters*, September 21, 2015, https://www.yahoo.com/news/burkina-armed-forces-move-capital-disarm-presidential-guard-143755435.html.

Boserup, A. and Mack, A. (1974). *War Without Weapons: Nonviolence in National Defence*. London: Frances Pinter.

Burrowes, Robert J. (1996). *The Strategy of Nonviolent Defense: A Gandhian Approach*. Albany, NY: SUNY Press.

Callahan, William, A. (1998). Imaging Democracy: Reading "the events of May" in Thailand. Singapore: Institute of South East Asian Studies.

Carasick, Lauren, "Honduras' political violence threatens to undermine its November elections," *Al Jazeera*, November 3, 2013, http://america.aljazeera.com/articles/2013/11/3/honduras-electionspoliticalviolence.html.

Chaffee, Lyman G. (1993). *Political Protest and Street Art: Popular Tools for Democratization in Latin America.* Greenwood.

Chenoweth, Erica and Maria J. Stephan (2011). *Why Civil Resistance Works: The Strategic Logic of Nonviolent Conflict.* New York: Columbia University Press.

Da Silva, P. Jose Luis, "Venezuelan Democracy in the 20th Century: The Struggle Between the Miliday and the Non-Military," *Politeja,* May 1, 2013.

Drosdoff, Daniel, "Disgruntled officers protesting human rights trials ended a three-day rebelion," April 17, 1987, *UPI,* http://www.upi.com/Archives/1987/04/17/Disgruntled-officers-protesting-human-rights-trials-ended-a-three-day/6372545630400/?spt=su.

Drosdoff, Daniel, "Alfonsin Used People Power to Defeat Revolt," April 20, 1987, *UPI,* https://www.upi.com/Archives/1987/04/20/Alfonsin-used-people-power-to-defeat-revolt/3047545889600/.

Dunne, Michele and Williamson, Scott, "Egypt's Unprecedented Instability by the Numbers" *Carnegie Endowment for International Peace.* March 24, 2014, http://carnegieendowment.org/2014/03/24/egypt-s-unprecedented-instability-by-numbers-pub-55078.

Eglitis, Ologerts (1992). *Nonviolent Action in the Liberation of Latvia* (Albert Einstein Institution Monograph Series #5). Cambridge, MA: The Albert Einstein Institution.

Flynn, Daniel, "Burkina Faso presidential guard seize president and PM". *Reuters,* September 16, 2015, http://www.reuters.com/article/us-burkina-army-idUSKCN0RG2HZ20150916.

Fort, Patrick and Romaric Ollo Hien, "Mooted amnesty deal for Burkina coup leaders branded 'shameful'", *Agence France-Presse,* September 20, 2015, https://www.yahoo.com/news/burkina-mediators-propose-return-president-amnesty-putchists-203558138.html.

Fort, Patrick and Romaric Ollo Hien, "Burkina president resumes power after week-long coup", *Agence France-Presse,* September 23, 2015, https://www.yahoo.com/news/burkinas-interim-leader-says-resuming-power-coup-101202420.html.

Franklin, Stephen, "In Egypt, Arab World's 'Largest Social Movement' Gains Steam Among Workers," *In These Times,* June 28, 2010.

Galván, Javier A. (2013). *Latin American Dictators of the 20th Century: The Lives and Regimes of 15 Rulers,* London: McFarland & Co.

Hien, Romaric Ollo, "African Union suspends Burkina Faso, slaps sanctions on coup junta", *Agence France-Presse,* September 18, 2015, https://www.yahoo.com/

news/african-union-suspends-burkina-faso-over-military-coup-171407973.html.

Huxley, S.D. (1990). *Constitutionalist Insurgency in Finland: Finnish "Passive Resistance" Against Russification as a Case of Nonmilitary Struggle in the European Resistance Tradition*. Helsinki: Finnish Historical Society.

Jullian, Maud, "Burkina Faso army reaches capital to quell coup", *BBC News*, 22 September 2015. http://www.bbc.com/news/world-africa-34321961.

Kirkpatrick, David D., "International "Observers Find Egypt's Presidential Election Fell Short of Standards" *New York Times*, May 29, 2014, https://www.nytimes.com/2014/05/30/world/middleeast/international-observers-find-fault-with-egypt-vote.html?_r=2.

King-Hall, Stephen (1958). *Defence in the Nuclear Age*. London: Gollancz.

Kurukulasuriya, Lasanda. "Maldives Commission Report – will it bring calm or storm?" *Sunday Times*, September 2, 2012, http://www.sundaytimes.lk/120902/columns/maldives-commission-report-will-it-bring-calm-or-storm-10614.html.

La Septieme Wilaya, "Egypt: Debunking the Egyptian Military Narrative of Popular Uprising", July 14, 2013, https://laseptiemewilaya.wordpress.com/2013/07/14/egypt-debunking-the-egyptian-military-narrative-of-popular-uprising-how-egyptians-did-really-protest-morsi-on-the-june-30th-protests/.

Le Monde Afrique, "Burkina Faso : le président et le premier ministre retenus par des militaires En savoir plus sur," September 16, 2015, http://www.lemonde.fr/afrique/article/2015/09/16/burkina-faso-le-president-et-le-premier-ministre-retenus-par-des-militaires_4759872_3212.html.

Martin, Brian (2007). *Justice Ignited: The Dynamics of Backfire*. Lanham, MD: Rowman & Littlefield.

Miniotaite, Grazina (2002). *Nonviolent Resistance in Lithuania: A Story of Peaceful Liberation* (Albert Einstein Institution Monograph Series #8). Boston, MA: The Albert Einstein Institution.

Naseem, Azra, "Coni and the Coupe: Constructing the Truth" *Dhivehi Sitee*, September 22, 2012, http://www.dhivehisitee.com/executive/making-coup-legal/.

Nelson, Bret, "Even When Coups Fail, the Effects Often Linger for Years," *Freedom House*, April 4, 2016, https://freedomhouse.org/blog/even-when-coups-fail-effects-often-linger-years.

Nepstad, Sharon Erickson (2011). *Nonviolent Revolutions: Civil Resistance in the Late 20th Century*. New York: Oxford University Press.

Ouedraogo, Brahima, "Burkina Faso junta frees interim president after coup", *Associated Press*, September 18, 2015.

Ouedraogo, Brahima, "Burkina Faso mediators propose November vote after coup", *Associated Press*, September 20, 2015.

Pew Research Center, "Egyptians Increasingly Glum", May 16, 2013, http://www.pewglobal.org/2013/05/16/egyptians-increasingly-glum/.

Powell, Jonathan M., and Clayton L. Thyne (2011). "Global Instances of Coups from 1950 to 2010: A New Dataset." *Journal of Peace Research* 48(2).

Radio Netherlands Worldwide, "Heroin Flooding the Maldives", https://www.rnw.org/archive/heroin-flooding-maldives.

Roberts, Adam (ed.) (1968). *Civilian Resistance as a National Defence: Non-violent Action Against Aggression*. Harrisburg, PA: Stackpole Books. (Originally published as The Strategy of Civilian Defence, London, Faber and Faber, 1967).

Roberts, Adam "Civil Resistance to Military Coups," *Journal of Peace Research*, 1975; 12; 19-36.

Russell, Bertrand (1915). "War and Non-Resistance" *Atlantic Monthly*, Vol. 116, No. 2 (August) 266–274.

Scheina, Robert L. (2003). *Latin America's Wars Volume II: The Age of the Professional Soldier*, 1900-2001.

Schmid, Alex (1985). *Social Defence and Soviet Military Power: An Inquiry into the Relevance of an Alternative Defence Concept*. Leiden: Center for the Study of Social Conflict, State University of Leiden.

Schock, Kurt (2005). *Unarmed Insurrections: People Power Movements in Nondemocracies*. Minneapolis: University of Minnesota Press.

Sharp, Gene (1973). *The Politics of Nonviolent Action*. Boston: Porter Sargent.

Sharp, Gene (1965). *The Political Equivalent of War: Civil Defense*. New York: Carnegie Endowment for International Peace.

Sharp, Gene (1985). *Making Europe Unconquerable: The Potential of Civilian-Based Deterrence and Defense*. Cambridge, MA: Ballinger Publishing Company.

Sharp, Gene (1990). *Civilian-Based Defense: A Post-Military System*. Princeton NJ: Princeton University Press.

Sharp, Gene and Bruce Jenkins (2003). *The Anti Coup*. Boston: Albert Einstein Institution).

Singh, Naunihal (2014). *Seizing Power: The Strategic Logic of Military Coups*.

Baltimore: Johns Hopkins University Press).

Solomon, Andrew, "At the Barricade," *The Moth*, http://player.themoth.org/#/?actionType=ADD_AND_PLAY&storyId=558.

Taoko, Herve, "An apology and a vow to end Burkina Faso coup", *New York Times*, September 21, 2015.

Tarrow, Sidney (1998). *Power in Movement*, second edition. Cambridge: Cambridge University Press.

Trinkunas, Harold A. (2005). *Crafting Civilian Control of the Military in Venezuela: A Comparative Perspective*. Chapel Hill: University of North Carolina Press.

UNDOC, "Intentional homicide, counts and rates per 100,000 population, 2015 https://data.unodc.org/#state:1

Vickers, George, "The Sham Elections in Honduras," *Foreign Policy*, November 29, 2009.

Weisbrot, Mark, "Honduran Elections Marred by Police Violence, Censorship, International Non-Recognition," *Truthout*, November 30, 2009.

Weissert, Will, "Exiled Honduran president vows return on Sunday". *Associated Press*, July 4, 2009.

Wsws.org "This Week In History: April 9-15", April 9, 2012, https://www.wsws.org/en/articles/2012/04/twih-a09.html.

Youssef, Ahmed Magdy, "Egypt Shuts Down More Media Channels". *Open Democracy*. October 2, 2013, https://www.opendemocracy.net/arab-awakening/ahmed-magdy-youssef/egypt-shuts-down-more-media-channels.

Zogby Research Services, "ZRS Releases September 2013 Egypt Poll". November 26, 2013, http://www.zogbyresearchservices.com/blog/2013/11/26/zrs-releases-september-2013-egypt-poll.

List of Scenarios and Tables

Scenario 1 14
Scenario 2 15
Scenario 3 15
Scenario 4 15
Scenario 5 16
Scenario 6 16
Table 1 — Soviet Union, 1991 26
Table 2 — Thailand, 1992 29
Table 3 — France, 1961 34
Table 4 — Argentina, 1987 38
Table 5 — Bolivia, 1978 43
Table 6 — Burkina Faso, 2015 48
Table 7 — Venezuela, 1958 54
Table 8 — Mali, 1991 59
Table 9 — Sudan, 1985 and 1989 64
Table 10 — Egypt, 2011 and 2013 69
Table 11 — Honduras, 2009 75
Table 12 — The Maldives, 2012 79
Table 13 — Twelve Case Studies Compared 82-88
Table 14 — Democratic Gains Estimate 91